The International Legal Framework on Violence Against Women

This book provides in-depth critical analysis of the international legal framework on violence against women and, crucially, the need for reform of this framework. Violence against women occurs in every state worldwide and constitutes one of the most prevalent human rights abuses at the global level. However, none of the UN treaties refer specifically to violence against women. The book argues that there is a pressing need for legally binding provisions to be adopted at the global level on this issue. Two forms which such provisions could take are considered. These are, firstly, an Optional Protocol to the UN Convention on the Elimination of All Forms of Discrimination Against Women; and secondly, a stand-alone UN treaty on violence against women. The book's intended audience includes academics and researchers from a wide variety of disciplines, such as human rights, international law, criminal law, criminology, social policy, gender studies and sociology; as well as practitioners and those in the voluntary sector who are working in the area of combating violence against women. The book could also be used beneficially on courses at both undergraduate and postgraduate levels which incorporate the topic of violence against women.

Ronagh J.A. McQuigg is Reader in the School of Law, Queen's University Belfast. Her research interests are in the area of international human rights law, and she currently teaches in the areas of Land Law and Family Law.

Routledge Research in Human Rights Law

Refugee Displacement, Disability and Human Rights
The Production, Processing and Power of Data
Philippa Duell-Piening

Detention and the Right to Liberty
Addressing Gaps in Protection at the European Court of Human Rights
Sabina Garahan

Transitional Justice Archives
Documenting Human Rights Violations in Latin America
Edited by Anita Ferrara and Beatrice Canossi

Hate Speech and the European Court of Human Rights
Natalie Alkiviadou

The Human Rights Principle of Indivisibility
Dorothea Anthony

Human Rights and Gender Based Violence in Asia
A Comparative Critical Analysis
Edited by Fozia Nazir Lone, Guobin Zhu, and Anthony Carty

Political Disinformation and the Law
Safeguarding Freedom of Expression in Europe
Christopher Phiri

The International Legal Framework on Violence Against Women
The Need for Reform
Ronagh J.A. McQuigg

For more information about this series, please visit: www.routledge.com/Routledge-Research-in-Human-Rights-Law/book-series/HUMRIGHTSLAW

The International Legal Framework on Violence Against Women

The Need for Reform

Ronagh J.A. McQuigg

Routledge
Taylor & Francis Group
LONDON AND NEW YORK

First published 2026
by Routledge
4 Park Square, Milton Park, Abingdon, Oxon OX14 4RN

and by Routledge
605 Third Avenue, New York, NY 10158

Routledge is an imprint of the Taylor & Francis Group, an informa business

British Library Cataloguing-in-Publication Data
A catalogue record for this book is available from the British Library

ISBN: 978-1-032-99353-9 (hbk)
ISBN: 978-1-032-99355-3 (pbk)
ISBN: 978-1-003-60368-9 (ebk)

DOI: 10.4324/9781003603689

Typeset in Times New Roman
by Apex CoVantage, LLC

Contents

1 Introduction

Violence against women occurs in every state worldwide and constitutes one of the most prevalent human rights abuses at the global level. According to the World Health Organization (WHO), around 30 per cent of women globally have been subjected to intimate partner violence or non-partner sexual violence in their lifetime. Most of this abuse consists of intimate partner violence. Almost one third of women aged 15–49 years who have been in a relationship report that they have been subjected to some form of violence by their partner. Up to 38 per cent of all murders of women globally are committed by intimate partners.[1] This book seeks to provide an in-depth critical analysis of the international legal framework on violence against women and argues that there a strong need for reform of this framework.

None of the United Nations (UN) treaties refers specifically to violence against women. This fact is all the more surprising given that since 1979 a 'women's convention', the UN Convention on the Elimination of All Forms of Discrimination Against Women (CEDAW), has been in existence. The monitoring body of CEDAW, the UN Committee on the Elimination of Discrimination Against Women (the CEDAW Committee), has nevertheless sought to include the issue of violence against women within its remit by interpreting various provisions of the Convention in such a manner as to encompass this issue.[2]

Other UN bodies have also addressed the subject of violence against women, for example the UN General Assembly has passed Resolutions on

1 World Health Organization, 'Violence Against Women', 25 March 2024, available at https://www.who.int/news-room/fact-sheets/detail/violence-against-women.

2 Committee on the Elimination of Discrimination Against Women, General Recommendation No. 12, U.N. Doc. A/44/38 (1989); Committee on the Elimination of Discrimination Against Women, General Recommendation No. 19, U.N. Doc. A/47/38 (1992); and Committee on the Elimination of Discrimination Against Women, General Recommendation No. 35 on gender-based violence against women, updating General Recommendation No. 19, CEDAW/C/GC/35 (2017).

DOI: 10.4324/9781003603689-1

this topic, including the important Declaration on the Elimination of Violence Against Women.[3] Most notably the office of UN Special Rapporteur on violence against women, its causes and consequences, was created in 1994, with a mandate to

> seek and receive information on violence against women, its causes and consequences, from Governments, treaty bodies, specialized agencies, other special rapporteurs . . . [and] recommend measures, ways and means, at the national, regional and international level to eliminate violence against women and its causes, and to remedy its consequences.[4]

The key focus of this book is however on the need for reform of the international framework on violence against women. The book provides critical analysis of an issue which is particularly topical due to a call issued jointly by the current UN Special Rapporteur on violence against women along with two previous Special Rapporteurs for states to consider the adoption of an Optional Protocol to CEDAW on violence against women.[5] This book considers the potential merits of the adoption of such a Protocol, and also the difficulties which such a course of action may entail.

It is nevertheless arguable that a preferable method of reform of the international framework on violence against women would be the adoption of a stand-alone UN treaty on this issue. The adoption of a stand-alone treaty on violence against women with its own monitoring body would allow for much more detailed scrutiny of state responses to this issue. The book therefore also analyses the potential merits of such a course of action, and the challenges which may be posed by the adoption of a stand-alone treaty.

Overall, it is argued that there is a strong need for reform of the international framework on violence against women, ideally in the form of a stand-alone treaty on this issue. However, the book recognises that such a development may not be achievable for reasons of practicality, such as the resources which would be entailed and lack of political will. It is therefore argued that, despite the potential difficulties involved, the adoption of an Optional Protocol to CEDAW on violence against women would be a very meritorious development in terms of reforming the international legal framework on this issue.

3 General Assembly Resolution A/RES/48/104, 20 December 1993.

4 U.N. Commission on Human Rights, Resolution 1994/45, paras. 7(a) and (b).

5 Statement by current and former Special Rapporteurs on violence against women, its causes and consequences, 'Now Is the Time for an Optional Protocol to CEDAW on Violence Against Women and Girls', 7 December 2023, available at https://www.ohchr.org/sites/default/files/documents/issues/women/sr/statements/stm-op-vaw-sr-vaw-7-12-23.pdf.

Chapter Outline

Chapter Two will set out the current international legal framework on violence against women. The chapter will explain that none of the UN human rights treaties refer specifically to violence against women, and that there are no legally binding treaty provisions at the global level which address this issue. Potential reasons for the omission from CEDAW of express reference to violence against women will be offered, such as the fact that this instrument was adopted 45 years ago, at a time when there was less of an understanding of the nature and prevalence of such violence. Importantly, human rights were originally formulated in such a manner as to create a 'public/private divide', whereby rights were deemed to be applicable in the 'public' sphere where the state was directly involved, but were not deemed to apply in the 'private' sphere in situations involving only private individuals.[6] As the majority of violence against women occurs in the 'private' sphere, the existence of the public/private dichotomy meant that such violence was largely excluded from the rights discourse. Although concepts of state responsibility and positive obligations have now been developed which enable human rights to enter the 'private' sphere,[7] such concepts were still in their infancy at the time of the drafting of CEDAW. In addition, although CEDAW has been described as an international bill of rights for women, it must be remembered that technically the aim of this instrument was to combat discrimination against women, as opposed to securing the rights of women more substantively. At the time of the drafting of CEDAW, violence against women was not generally viewed as a matter relating to gender-based discrimination as such.

Nevertheless, as will also be discussed in Chapter Two, despite the omission from CEDAW of any express reference to violence against women, the CEDAW Committee has however in its General Recommendations Nos. 19 and 35 interpreted this instrument in such a way as to encompass this issue.[8] In addition, statements addressing the subject of violence against women made by other UN bodies will be examined in this chapter.

6 See further, Romany, C., 'Women as Aliens: A Feminist Critique of the Public/Private Distinction in International Human Rights Law' (1993) 6 *Harvard Human Rights Journal* 87.

7 See further, Fredman, S., *Human Rights Transformed – Positive Rights and Positive Duties*, 2009, Oxford University Press, Oxford; Ewing, A.P., 'Establishing State Responsibility For Private Acts of Violence Against Women Under the American Convention on Human Rights' (1995) 26 *Columbia Human Rights Law Review* 751; and Mowbray, A.R., *The Development of Positive Obligations Under the European Convention on Human Rights by the European Court of Human Rights*, 2004, Hart Publishing, Oxford.

8 Committee on the Elimination of Discrimination Against Women, General Recommendation No. 19, U.N. Doc. A/47/38 (1992); and Committee on the Elimination of Discrimination Against Women, General Recommendation No. 35 on gender-based violence against women, updating General Recommendation No. 19, CEDAW/C/GC/35 (2017).

Chapter Three will examine why reform of the international legal framework on violence against women is needed. Although a multitude of statements have been issued by the CEDAW Committee and by other UN bodies on this issue, these all fall within the category of 'soft law' which is non-binding on states. This situation is potentially problematic from two perspectives. The first of these relates to whether it is acceptable from the perspective of principle that there are still no legally binding standards at the global level on the issue of violence against women. The second, and arguably even more crucial, aspect is more pragmatic in nature and centres on the argument that the absence of legally binding provisions at the global level on violence against women makes states less responsive to the need to adopt meaningful and effective measures in this area.

As regards the first aspect, the chapter will argue that it is problematic from the perspective of principle that there are no legally binding provisions on violence against women at the global level. When CEDAW was adopted in 1979, the prevalence and nature of violence against women was not understood to any great extent. However, since then there have been enormous developments in the understanding of this phenomenon, and it is now no longer tenable for the lack of UN treaty provisions on violence against women to remain unaddressed. Such provisions would have a symbolic value, demonstrating the importance of the issue of such violence. At present it appears that one almost has to twist CEDAW in order to attempt to make this instrument encompass the issue of violence against women, and it will be argued that the adoption of legally binding provisions at the global level would add substantially more force to the statements made by the CEDAW Committee and the other UN human rights bodies as regards this issue.

In relation to the second aspect, the chapter will consider whether the lack of legally binding provisions at the UN level on violence against women is also problematic from a practical perspective. This will involve discussion of two inter-related issues. These are, firstly, whether the existence of human rights standards actually makes a difference as regards the responses of states to particular issues; and secondly, if so, whether it matters in terms of state responses whether the human rights standards in question are legally binding or otherwise. Although there are of course considerable difficulties with the implementation of human rights standards,[9] the chapter will argue that the existence of such standards do make a significant difference as regards how

9 See further, Hafner-Burton, E.M. and Tsutsui, K., 'Human Rights in a Globalizing World: The Paradox of Empty Promises' (2005) 110 *American Journal of Sociology* 1373; Byrnes, A., 'Enforcement Through International Law and Procedures', in Cook, R.J. (ed.), *Human Rights of Women – National and International Perspectives*, 1994, University of Pennsylvania Press, Philadelphia, 189; and Crawford, J., 'The UN Human Rights Treaty System: A System in Crisis?', in Alston, P. and Crawford, J. (eds.), *The Future of UN Human Rights Treaty Monitoring*, 2000, Cambridge University Press, Cambridge, 1.

states respond to particular issues. It is also argued that human rights standards need to be legally binding in order for them to attain a sufficient degree of efficacy. On this point, it is notable that in 2011 the Council of Europe adopted the Convention on Preventing and Combating Violence Against Women and Domestic Violence (the Istanbul Convention),[10] and that in 2025 the African Union (AU) adopted the Convention on Ending Violence Against Women and Girls, despite the fact that all of the member states of both the Council of Europe and the African Union were already parties to CEDAW and were therefore subject to the 'soft law' standards developed by the CEDAW Committee and the other UN bodies in this area. Few of the measures found among the provisions of the Istanbul Convention or the AU Convention were new – most had been previously articulated by the CEDAW Committee and other UN bodies. However, the Council of Europe and the AU nevertheless saw fit to put these standards in the format of treaties, thereby making them legally binding. If the Council of Europe or the AU had been of the view that it was of no consequence whether these standards were merely 'soft law' or were of a legally binding nature, there would have been little or no point in adopting these Conventions.

Additionally, the chapter will argue that the fact that there are a number of legally binding provisions on violence against women within the context of regional systems of human rights protection by no means eliminates the need for legally binding provisions at the UN level on this issue. It must be remembered there are huge swathes of the globe which do not fall within any of the regional systems of human rights protection which encompass treaty provisions on violence against women. Also, the regional provisions on this issue which are currently in existence vary dramatically in terms of scope. For example, the Istanbul Convention places extremely extensive and detailed duties on states parties, whereas the AU Convention and the Inter-American Convention on the Prevention, Punishment and Eradication of Violence Against Women (the Convention of Belém do Pará), which was adopted three decades ago, place considerably less detailed obligations on states parties. There is thus a need for a uniform set of obligations to be adopted at the UN level.

Of course, it is recognised that the adoption of legally binding provisions at the UN level on violence against women would not be straightforward. The chapter will therefore also address potential problems and consider the extent to which it is likely that states would ratify a legally binding UN instrument on violence against women.

10 See further, McQuigg, R., *The Istanbul Convention, Domestic Violence and Human Rights*, 2017, Routledge, Abingdon; and De Vido, S. and Frulli, M. (eds.), *Preventing and Combating Violence Against Women and Domestic Violence: A Commentary on the Istanbul Convention*, 2023, Edward Elgar Publishing, Cheltenham.

Chapter Four will then address the first of two potential forms a legally binding instrument may take, namely an Optional Protocol to CEDAW on violence against women. The adoption of such an Optional Protocol, to be monitored by the CEDAW Committee, has certain attractions, in that this course of action would be likely to be substantially less costly than the adoption of a stand-alone treaty and the establishment of a separate monitoring body. In addition, this approach would carry less of a reporting burden for states, in that states parties to such a Protocol could include information on compliance within their reports to the CEDAW Committee on their implementation of CEDAW more generally.[11] This may in turn have the advantage of encouraging more states to ratify such an instrument. Furthermore, it is likely that the substantive content of an Optional Protocol on violence against women would be based largely on the CEDAW Committee's General Recommendation No. 35 on gender-based violence. The existence of this General Recommendation means that there would be an initial blueprint from which to work in terms of drafting such an Optional Protocol. The fact that the CEDAW Committee already refers to General Recommendation No. 35 when assessing state compliance with CEDAW may encourage states to ratify an Optional Protocol based on this General Recommendation, given that they would already have a level of familiarity with the provisions contained therein. As it is likely that an Optional Protocol would be based heavily on General Recommendation No. 35, Chapter Four will include analysis of the content of this General Recommendation.

The adoption of an Optional Protocol to CEDAW, as opposed to a stand-alone treaty, could also however carry significant disadvantages. The CEDAW Committee already works under considerable pressure, and it is difficult to see how this body could undertake any additional burden of monitoring. Given that the CEDAW Committee already refers to General Recommendation No. 35 in its Concluding Observations on state reports, it could be that the adoption of an Optional Protocol on violence against women would make little difference in practice, as the CEDAW Committee may well be unable to devote any additional time to monitoring state responses to violence against women in any greater depth than it does currently. Indeed, the rather odd situation could occur whereby states which have chosen not to ratify an Optional Protocol on violence against women could nevertheless be held to account, through the Committee's use of General Recommendation No. 35, as regards compliance with essentially the same obligations as states which have ratified such a Protocol. Alternatively, states which may choose not to ratify an Optional Protocol may seek to argue that the CEDAW Committee should not refer to General Recommendation No. 35 when assessing

11 Under Article 18 of CEDAW, states parties must submit periodic reports regarding their compliance with this instrument for consideration by the CEDAW Committee.

their compliance with CEDAW, given that they are not party to similar obligations contained in a Protocol. It is not inconceivable that this could lead to some states making lesser attempts to address violence against women than they do at present.

Chapter Five will therefore proceed to examine another form which legally binding provisions at the UN level on violence against women could take, namely a stand-alone treaty on violence against women. By contrast to an Optional Protocol to CEDAW, the adoption of a stand-alone UN treaty on violence against women with its own monitoring body would allow for much more detailed scrutiny of state responses to this issue. As will be discussed in Chapter Five, this point is brought into particularly sharp focus when a comparison is made between monitoring of state compliance with the Istanbul Convention and the monitoring of state responses to violence against women as carried out by the CEDAW Committee. It is of course unlikely for reasons of practicality that the very thorough approach to monitoring state compliance with the Istanbul Convention, which has currently been ratified by 38 states, could be replicated in the context of a global treaty with potentially a far greater number of states parties.[12] Nevertheless, a monitoring body focused solely on violence against women would be able to assess compliance in a more detailed manner than the CEDAW Committee, the capacity of which is already over-stretched, could assess compliance with a new Optional Protocol to CEDAW. In addition, the adoption of a new UN treaty on violence against women would allow for considerably greater flexibility in terms of the monitoring mechanisms which would pertain to such an instrument, as will also be explored in Chapter Five.

Chapter Six will summarise the key points and conclusions from the preceding discussion. The chapter will also include reflections on the most probable form which legally binding provisions at the global level on violence against women could take. This book argues that it would be best for such standards to be implemented in the form of a new stand-alone treaty on violence against women. It is however recognised that, given that the current UN Special Rapporteur on violence against women and two previous holders of this role have expressed their support for an Optional Protocol to CEDAW on violence against women, it is now very unlikely that the more radical alternative of a stand-alone instrument would be adopted. Nevertheless, even though an Optional Protocol to CEDAW on violence against women would not offer the same opportunities for innovative monitoring methods or in-depth scrutiny of state compliance as would a stand-alone treaty with its own monitoring body, the potential significance of such an Optional Protocol should not be underestimated. The adoption of such an instrument would have tremendous symbolic value in terms of a recognition at the international level of the

12 For example, there are currently 189 states parties to CEDAW.

prevalence and importance of the issue of violence against women and of the urgent need for further steps to be taken to address this issue. Such an Optional Protocol would also add substantially more force to the statements made by the CEDAW Committee and the other UN human rights bodies regarding violence against women. Although the ideal way forward may have been the adoption of a stand-alone treaty, idealism must at times give way to realism and to a recognition that compromise may be necessary. To that end, it is to be hoped that the UN bodies and states parties will work together to develop and implement an Optional Protocol to CEDAW on violence against women.

2 The International Legal Framework on Violence Against Women

Chapter Two sets out the current international legal framework on violence against women. The chapter explains that none of the UN human rights treaties refer specifically to violence against women, and that there are no legally binding treaty provisions at the global level which address this issue. Potential reasons for the omission from CEDAW of express reference to violence against women are offered, such as the fact that this instrument was adopted 45 years ago, at a time when there was less understanding of the importance and prevalence of such violence. Also, human rights were originally formulated in such a manner as to create a 'public/private divide', whereby rights were deemed to be applicable in the 'public' sphere where the state was directly involved, but were not deemed to apply in the 'private' sphere in situations involving only private individuals. As the majority of violence against women occurs in the 'private' sphere, the existence of the public/private dichotomy meant that such violence was largely excluded from the rights discourse. Although concepts of state responsibility and positive obligations have now been developed which enable human rights to enter the 'private' sphere, such concepts were still in their infancy at the time of the drafting of CEDAW. In addition, although CEDAW has been described as an international bill of rights for women, it must be remembered that technically the aim of this instrument was to combat discrimination against women, as opposed to securing the rights of women more substantively. At the time of the drafting of CEDAW, violence against women was not generally viewed as a matter relating to gender-based discrimination as such.

Nevertheless, despite the omission from CEDAW of any express reference to violence against women, the CEDAW Committee has however in its General Recommendations Nos. 19 and 35 interpreted this instrument in such a way as to encompass this issue,[1] as is discussed in this chapter. Other

1 Committee on the Elimination of Discrimination Against Women, General Recommendation No. 19, U.N. Doc. A/47/38 (1992); and Committee on the Elimination of Discrimination Against Women, General Recommendation No. 35 on gender-based violence against women, updating General Recommendation No. 19, CEDAW/C/GC/35 (2017).

DOI: 10.4324/9781003603689-2

UN bodies have also addressed the subject of violence against women. For instance, the UN General Assembly has passed Resolutions on this issue, including the important UN Declaration on the Elimination of Violence Against Women.[2] Resolutions relating to violence against women were also issued by the Commission on Human Rights,[3] and have been issued by the Human Rights Council, which replaced the Commission on Human Rights in 2006.[4] In addition, violence against women was addressed in the Vienna Declaration and Programme of Action which was adopted by the World Conference on Human Rights in Vienna in June 1993. Indeed the importance which is accorded by the UN bodies to this subject is seen in the very existence of the office of the Special Rapporteur on violence against women, its causes and consequences. Since the inception of this post in 1994, those who have held the office have issued a multitude of detailed reports. In addition, the Beijing Declaration and Platform for Action, which was issued following the Fourth World Conference on Women organised by the UN and took place in 1995, contained detailed recommendations on the measures which states should adopt in order to address violence against women.[5]

The Omission of Violence Against Women From CEDAW

CEDAW was adopted in 1979 by the UN General Assembly and entered into force in 1981. The Convention essentially defines what constitutes discrimination against women and sets out what national action should be taken to end such discrimination.[6] In Article 1 of CEDAW, discrimination against women is defined as

> any distinction, exclusion or restriction made on the basis of sex which has the effect or purpose of impairing or nullifying the recognition, enjoyment

2 General Assembly Resolution A/RES/48/104, 20 December 1993. See also for example, the Resolutions of the General Assembly on intensification of efforts to eliminate all forms of violence against women which were adopted on 19 December 2006 (A/RES/61/143); 18 December 2007 (A/RES/62/133); 18 December 2008 (A/RES/63/155); 18 December 2009 (A/RES/64/137); 21 December 2010 (A/RES/65/187); 20 December 2012 (A/RES/67/144).

3 See for example Commission on Human Rights Resolution E/CN.4/RES/2001/49, 23 April 2001; Commission on Human Rights Resolution E/CN.4/RES/2004/46, 20 April 2004.

4 See for example Resolution 7/24 (2008) 'Elimination of Violence Against Women'; Resolution 11/2 (2009) 'Accelerating Efforts to Eliminate All Forms of Violence Against Women'; Resolution 14/12 (2010) 'Accelerating Efforts to Eliminate All Forms of Violence Against Women: Ensuring Due Diligence in Prevention'; Resolution 20/12 (2012) 'Accelerating Efforts to Eliminate All Forms of Violence Against Women: Remedies for Women Who Have Been Subjected to Violence'.

5 Beijing Platform for Action, U.N. Doc. A/CONF. 177/20 (1995).

6 For discussion of CEDAW generally, see Chinkin, C. and Freeman, M.A., 'Introduction', in Freeman, M.A., Chinkin, C. and Rudolf, B. (eds.), *The UN Convention on the Elimination of*

> or exercise by women, irrespective of their marital status, on a basis of equality of men and women, of human rights and fundamental freedoms in the political, economic, social, cultural, civil or any other field.

At the time of writing, 189 states are parties to CEDAW. This means that it is one of the most widely ratified of the UN treaties. However, it is important to note that this instrument contains no express mention of violence against women within its provisions. Given that CEDAW is largely understood as being an international bill of rights for women, it may seem somewhat surprising that this instrument contains no express reference to the issue of violence against women, given that such violence constitutes one of the most prevalent human rights abuses globally. As the CEDAW Committee itself comments, 'gender-based violence against women . . . remains pervasive in all countries of the world, with high levels of impunity'.[7] Rehman remarks, 'A serious criticism of the Women's Convention has been the absence of specific provisions condemning violence against women, an omission which is unacceptable in the light of everyday instances of violence against women in every region of the world'.[8]

It must nevertheless be remembered that CEDAW was adopted by the UN General Assembly around 45 years ago in 1979 and entered into force in 1981. Understandings of violence against women have developed greatly since the inception of this instrument. For instance, it is now widely recognised that domestic abuse constitutes one of the most prevalent forms of violence against women. However, it was only in the 1970s that domestic abuse was even recognised as constituting a significant social problem,[9] let alone an issue which needed to be addressed by legal measures. As Burton comments, 'Until the 1970s there was little recognition of domestic violence as an issue that ought to be tackled by the legal system', even at the national level.[10] Indeed, domestic abuse was not recognised as constituting 'a significant social problem' until this time.[11] Even after it became clear in some quarters that legal intervention was crucial as regards this issue, actors within the criminal justice system, such as police, prosecutors and courts, continued to display a reluctance to treat violence taking place in the home as being on a par with

---

All Forms of Discrimination Against Women – A Commentary, 2012, Oxford University Press, Oxford, 2; and Byrnes, A., 'The Convention on the Elimination of All Forms of Discrimination Against Women', in Benedek, W., Mayambala Kisaakye, E. and Oberleitner, G. (eds.), *Human Rights of Women: International Instruments and African Experiences*, 2002, Palgrave, New York, 119.

7 General Recommendation No. 35, at para. 6.

8 Rehman, J., *International Human Rights Law*, 2nd ed., 2010, Pearson Education Limited, Harlow, 551.

9 Burton, M., *Legal Responses to Domestic Violence*, 2008, Routledge-Cavendish, Abingdon, 11.

10 Burton, op. cit., 2.

11 Burton, op. cit., 11.

violence occurring in other circumstances.[12] Dobash and Dobash state, 'In the early 1970s, activists discovered what battered women had long known, that the (criminal justice system) failed to protect the victim or to act against the offender'.[13] Indeed Radford, writing in 1987, commented that solicitors would frequently discourage victims of domestic abuse from seeking legal remedies. Radford was of the view that such attitudes among solicitors may have been due to some solicitors being unsympathetic to victims of domestic abuse and assuming that it was the victims who had precipitated any violence which had occurred.[14]

Many commentators have argued that unhelpful police attitudes constituted a very significant problem as regards domestic abuse. For example, writing in 1997, Armatta stated, 'police throughout the world often fail to enforce criminal assault laws where violence occurs within an intimate relationship. Traditionally, police simply do not intervene, or intervene only to mediate on an informal basis'.[15] In 2003, Sullivan commented that police could not be relied upon to arrest the perpetrator.[16] In 2006, Hughes remarked, 'Police forces may be unresponsive to requests for assistance from women on the receiving end of domestic violence, or they may adopt a non-interventionist approach, considering that it is a "private" matter'.[17]

Research carried out in the UK during the late 1970s and early 1980s demonstrated the unhelpful attitudes of the police towards victims of domestic abuse at this time. For example, in the report of research carried out by the University of Bradford in 1979, it was stated, 'a man's home is his castle, and very little short of murdering his wife will make people feel justified in violating its privacy'.[18] Essentially, violence against women taking place in the home was viewed as being unlike other types of criminal behaviour, and even not truly 'criminal' in nature. The study found that the police were extremely reluctant to violate the privacy of a perpetrator of domestic abuse by intervening in the situation to protect his wife or partner. Dobash and Dobash also

12 See also McQuigg, R., *International Human Rights Law and Domestic Violence*, 2011, Routledge, Abingdon, 19–30.

13 Dobash, R.E. and Dobash, R.P., *Women, Violence and Social Change*, 1992, Routledge, New York, 141.

14 Radford, L., 'Legalising Woman Abuse', in Hanmer, J. and Maynard, M. (eds.), *Women, Violence and Social Control*, 1987, Macmillan, London, 135. See also Burton, op. cit., 33–35.

15 Armatta, J., 'Getting Beyond the Law's Complicity in Intimate Violence Against Women' (1997) 33 *Willamette Law Review* 774 at 812.

16 Sullivan, C.M., 'Using the ESID Model to Reduce Intimate Male Violence Against Women' (2003) 32 *American Journal of Community Psychology* 295 at 296.

17 Hughes, B., 'Can Domestic Violence be Considered a Violation of Human Rights Law?' (2006) 14 *British Journal of Midwifery* 192.

18 Bruce, E., 'Attitudes of Social Workers and Police in the Select Committee Report on Violence to Women and Children', in *Women and Abused Children – Intricacies of Legal and Administrative Intervention*, 1979, Issues Publications, University of Bradford, 50–61 at 53.

carried out research in 1979 into police responses to domestic abuse, and they too found that responses were typified by 'animosity or at best indifference'.[19]

A study carried out by the Research and Planning Unit of the Home Office in 1989 uncovered similar findings. In the report of the study it was commented that 'the single most common police response is non-intervention, that is, officers state that there is nothing they can do and leave the incident to which they have been called.'[20] The report stated that a frequent occurrence was for the victim to be told that the abuse she had suffered was a matter for the civil and not the criminal law. This was in line with general attitudes whereby domestic abuse was regarded as being not truly 'criminal' in character. Other responses remarked upon by the Home Office study included attempts to defuse the situation and the removal of one of the parties from the scene for a period of time. Notably, it was often the victim who was removed.[21] Another study carried out in 1989, by Edwards, found that there was a substantial reluctance among police to record domestic abuse as a crime. As with the Home Office study, Edwards found that police would frequently encourage the victim to use civil remedies, even when the victim wished for the perpetrator to be arrested.[22]

The view of domestic abuse as not being criminal in nature was, as the Home Office study pointed out, based on the idea that 'domestic violence is almost exclusively a "family matter" or a "private affair" in which State intervention has no business since it would constitute not solely an intrusion into a private relationship but also an erosion of individual liberties'.[23] Edwards was of the view that inadequate police responses resulted from 'private attitudes regarding appropriate sex roles, appropriate conduct and family ideologies'.[24] Writing in 1990, Boulet commented, 'most officers had a negative attitude towards marital violence, often feeling that they should not become involved'.[25] Goodmark asserts that in the United States also, 'Police officers frequently told abusive spouses to take a walk around the block to cool down and attempted to mediate between abusers and their victims'.[26]

19 Dobash, R.E. and Dobash, R.P., *Violence Against Wives: A Case Against the Patriarchy*, 1979, Open Books, London, 191.

20 Smith, L.J.F., 'Domestic Violence: An Overview of the Literature' [1989] *Home Office Research Study* 107, 47.

21 Smith, op. cit., 47.

22 Edwards, S., *Policing 'Domestic' Violence: Women, the Law and the State*, 1989, Sage Publications, London.

23 Smith, op. cit.55.

24 Edwards, op. cit., 91.

25 Bourlet, A., *Police Intervention in Marital Violence*, 1990, Open University Press, Milton Keynes, 74.

26 Goodmark, L., 'Symposium: Domestic Violence & the Law: Theory, Policy, and Practice: Law is the Answer? Do We Know that for Sure?: Questioning the Efficacy of Legal Interventions for Battered Women' (2004) 23 *Saint Louis University Public Law Review* 7 at 13.

It took even longer for violence against women to be recognised as an issue for international human rights law.[27] Part of the difficulty related to understandings of the discourse of human rights. International relations are founded upon the concept of the liberal state. Romany remarks, 'Liberalism constructs a social and political order which seeks to emancipate the individual from the oppression of political structures'.[28] International law therefore has its basis in the liberal social contract theory, whereby states are viewed as individuals which should have equality, independence and freedom. Inherent to this theory is the concept of negative rights ensuring individual freedom. This idea is therefore embedded deeply in the discourse of international law, and subsequently human rights law.[29] Essentially the concept of 'negative rights' means that the state cannot interfere with an individual in certain aspects of his or her life.[30] As Fredman remarks, 'Human rights have long been understood as providing protection for individual freedom against an intrusive State.'[31] Another main principle of international law is that in general only states can be subject to this body of law.

The concept of negative rights ensuring individual freedoms emerged again during the fight against totalitarianism, which constituted an important catalyst in the development of human rights law. Human rights evolved to protect the rights of the individual from encroachment by the state. As Thomas and Beasley comment, 'States are bound by international law to respect the individual rights of each and every person and are thus accountable for abuses of those rights'.[32] However, the rights norms which emerged were generally formulated in a negative way, whereby the state was obliged only to refrain from breaching the rights in question. There were no duties on the state to adopt positive measures to ensure that the rights of the individual were not violated. In addition, the 'neo-liberal commitment to minimal state intervention'[33] resulted in the situation whereby the state was not obliged to protect the rights of the individual from violation by another private party.

Rights therefore developed in such a way as to create a public/private divide by which human rights norms were upheld in the public sphere where

27 See also McQuigg, op. cit., 3–8.

28 Romany, C., 'Women as Aliens: A Feminist Critique of the Public/Private Distinction in International Human Rights Law' (1993) 6 *Harvard Human Rights Journal* 87 at 90.

29 Romany, op. cit., 89–98.

30 For historical arguments on rights, see Harvey, C., 'Talking About Human Rights' [2004] *European Human Rights Law Review* 500.

31 Fredman, S., *Human Rights Transformed – Positive Rights and Positive Duties*, 2009, Oxford University Press, Oxford, 1.

32 Thomas, D.Q. and Beasley, M.E., 'Symposium on Reconceptualizing Violence Against Women by Intimate Partners' (1995) 58 *Albany Law Review* 1119 at 1121.

33 Hirschl, R., '"Negative" Rights vs. "Positive" Entitlements: A Comparative Study of Judicial Interpretations of Rights in an Emerging Neo-Liberal Economic Order' (2000) 22 *Human Rights Quarterly* 1060 at 1063.

the state was involved, but were not applied in the private sphere. Violence against women tends to occur largely in what was viewed as constituting the private sphere. The public/private dichotomy may be formulated in several ways. Cook highlights two possibilities.[34] Firstly, the public sphere can be viewed as the area which is regulated by law and politics, and the private sphere as the area where regulation is seen as inappropriate. Secondly, the public realm can be viewed as the state and its agents, while the private arena is constituted by non-state activities. As regards the first formulation of the public/private dichotomy, it is true that many would be of the view that there are certain areas which should remain unregulated, in order to respect the right to privacy. However, the public/private divide has been applied to, for example, the issue of domestic abuse in a manner which is extremely problematic. As Burton comments, 'In the classic public/private dichotomy intimate relationships are seen as part of the "private" sphere not suitable for public regulation'.[35] Indeed it has been attitudes such as this which have created such immense difficulties historically regarding the responses of actors within the criminal justice system to cases of domestic abuse, as was discussed earlier in the chapter.

The second formulation of the public/private divide, as outlined by Cook, is equally problematic. As Ewing comments, 'The public/private distinction in international law . . . places many forms of violence against women beyond the protective scope of human rights instruments'.[36] The rights of women often come into conflict with powers other than that of the state. These powers generally emanate from the private arena, such as from within the family unit.[37] Knop states, 'women are more vulnerable than men to serious harm, injustice, and discrimination in the private sphere, and the public/private distinction has prevented the law from remedying the situation'.[38] Women all around the globe suffer from violence occurring in the private sphere such as, for example, domestic abuse, female genital mutilation and dowry killing.[39] Under traditional principles, such abuses did not come within the scope of

34 Cook, R.J., 'Women's International Human Rights Law: The Way Forward', in Cook, R.J. (ed.), *Human Rights of Women – National and International Perspectives*, 1994, University of Pennsylvania Press, Philadelphia, 3 at 6.

35 Burton, op. cit., 7. See also Lacey, N., *Unspeakable Subjects*, 1998, Hart Publishing, Oxford, 71–97.

36 Ewing, A.P., 'Establishing State Responsibility For Private Acts of Violence Against Women Under the American Convention on Human Rights' (1995) 26 *Columbia Human Rights Law Review* 751 at 753.

37 Rishmawi, M., 'The Developing Approaches of the International Commission of Jurists to Women's Human Rights', in Cook, R.J. (ed.), *Human Rights of Women – National and International Perspectives*, 1994, University of Pennsylvania Press, Philadelphia, 340 at 341.

38 Knop, K., 'Introduction', in Knop, K. (ed.), *Gender and Human Rights*, 2004, Oxford University Press, Oxford, 1 at 6.

39 Rishmawi, op. cit., 341.

human rights law as they are not inflicted directly by the state. As Isa remarks, 'international human rights law and the set of international legal norms it encompasses has developed in such a way that it reflects the experiences of men, excluding those of women'.[40] Van Leeuwen comments, 'abuses, exclusions and constraints that are more typical of women's lives are neither recognised nor protected by mainstream human rights instruments'.[41] Charlesworth states that the main impact of the public/private dichotomy has been 'to muffle, and often completely silence, the voices of women'.[42]

The public/private divide does not however now pose an insurmountable problem as regards the recognition of violence against women occurring in the private sphere as falling within the ambit of international human rights law. Various methods have emerged through which human rights may now enter into the private sphere. In particular, the concept of state responsibility has been developed, under which positive obligations can be placed directly on the state to ensure that human rights standards are upheld in situations involving only private individuals. For example, the UN human rights bodies frequently refer to the state's duties to respect, protect, promote and fulfil rights. At the regional level, both the Inter-American Court on Human Rights and the European Court of Human Rights (ECtHR)[43] have been extremely

40 Isa, F.G., 'The Optional Protocol for the Convention on the Elimination of All Forms of Discrimination Against Women: Strengthening the Protection of Women's Human Rights' (2003) 20 *Arizona Journal of International and Comparative Law* 291 at 293.

41 Van Leeuwen, F., *Women's Rights Are Human Rights*, 2010, Intersentia, Antwerp, 9.

42 Charlesworth, H., 'What Are "Women's International Human Rights"?', in Cook, R.J. (ed.), *Human Rights of Women – National and International Perspectives*, 1994, University of Pennsylvania Press, Philadelphia, 58 at 68. For discussion of the rights of women in international human rights law, see Johnstone, R.L., 'Feminist Influences on the United Nations Human Rights Treaty Bodies' (2006) 28 *Human Rights Quarterly* 148; Charlesworth, H. and Chinkin, C., *The Boundaries of International Law: A Feminist Analysis*, 2000, Manchester University Press, Manchester; Binion, G., 'Human Rights: A Feminist Perspective' (1995) 17 *Human Rights Quarterly* 509; Fraser, A.S., 'Becoming Human: The Origin and Development of Women's Human Rights Law' (1999) 21 *Human Rights Quarterly* 853; Charlesworth, H., Chinkin, C. and Wright, S., 'Feminist Approaches to International Law' (1991) 85 *American Journal of International Law* 613; Bond, J.E., 'International Intersectionality: A Theoretical and Pragmatic Exploration of Women's International Human Rights Violations' (2003) 52 *Emory Law Journal* 71; Bunch, C., 'Women's Rights as Human Rights: Towards a Re-Visioning of Human Rights' (1990) 12 *Human Rights Quarterly* 486; O'Hare, U., 'Realising Women's Human Rights' (1999) 21 *Human Rights Quarterly* 364; Lacey, N., 'Feminist Legal Theory and the Rights of Women', in Knop, K. (ed.), *Gender and Human Rights*, 2004, Oxford University Press, Oxford, 13; and Gaer, F.D., 'And Never the Twain Shall Meet? The Struggle to Establish Women's Rights as International Human Rights', in Lockwood, C.E., Magraw, D.B., Spring, M.F. and Strong, S.I. (eds.), *The International Human Rights of Women – Instruments of Change*, 1998, American Bar Association, Washington, DC, 1.

43 See further, Mowbray, A.R., *The Development of Positive Obligations Under the European Convention on Human Rights by the European Court of Human Rights*, 2004, Hart Publishing, Oxford, 221.

instrumental in developing the concepts of state responsibility and positive obligations. Indeed the Inter-American Court on Human Rights is credited with one of the earliest formulations of the principle of state responsibility in the case of *Velasquez Rodriguez v Honduras*,[44] which concerned the disappearance of Manfredo Velasquez. In this case, the Inter-American Court held that Honduras had failed to fulfil its duties under Article 1(1) of the American Convention on Human Rights. The Court stated,

> An illegal act which violates human rights and which is initially not directly imputable to a State (for example, because it is the act of a private person or because the person responsible has not been identified) can lead to international responsibility of the State, not because of the act itself, but because of the lack of due diligence to prevent the violation or to respond to it as required by the Convention.[45]

The Court went on to assert that the duty of states to prevent violations,

> includes all those means of a legal, political, administrative and cultural nature that promote the protection of human rights and ensure that any violations are considered and treated as illegal acts, which, as such, may lead to the punishment of those responsible and the obligation to indemnify the victims for damages.[46]

However, this judgment was not issued until 1988, almost a decade after the adoption of CEDAW.

Essentially, as Edwards states, 'Prior to the 1990s . . . violence against women was not seen as a major issue, and if it was recognised as an issue at all, it was considered an issue for national governments (and criminal law) rather than international law'.[47] Given the prevalent understandings of both violence against women and human rights at the time of the drafting of CEDAW, it is perhaps to be expected that no express reference to violence against women is contained in this instrument.

There is also a further potential reason for the omission from CEDAW of any express reference to violence against women. Although CEDAW has been described as an international bill of rights for women, it must be remembered that technically the aim of this instrument was to combat discrimination against women, rather than securing the rights of women more substantively.

44 Judgment of 29 July 1988, Inter-Am. Ct. H.R., (Ser. C) No. 4.

45 At para. 172.

46 At para. 175.

47 Edwards, A., *Violence Against Women Under International Human Rights Law*, 2013, Cambridge University Press, Cambridge, 7.

Violence against women has of course now been recognised as an issue falling within the scope of anti-discrimination provisions. For example, since 2009 the ECtHR has found violations of Article 14 of the European Convention on Human Rights in cases involving domestic abuse.[48] Article 14 states,

> The enjoyment of the rights and freedoms set forth in this Convention shall be secured without discrimination on any ground such as sex, race, colour, language, religion, political or other opinion, national or social origin, association with a national minority, property, birth or other status.

Opuz v Turkey[49] was the first domestic abuse case before the ECtHR in which a breach of Article 14 was found. In this case, the applicant demonstrated through statistical data that domestic abuse affected mainly women and that judicial passivity in Turkey created a climate which was conducive to such abuse. In finding a violation of Article 14 taken in conjunction with Articles 2 (the right to life) and 3 (the right to be free from torture or inhuman or degrading treatment), the ECtHR stated,

> Bearing in mind . . . that the general and discriminatory judicial passivity in Turkey, albeit unintentional, mainly affected women, the Court considers that the violence suffered by the applicant and her mother may be regarded as gender-based violence which is a form of discrimination against women.[50]

Nevertheless, an anti-discrimination framework is perhaps not the most obvious discourse in terms of addressing violence against women. Instead, more substantive rights, such as the right to be free from torture or inhuman or

48 See *Opuz v Turkey* (App. No. 33401/02), judgment of 9 June 2009; *Eremia and Others v Moldova* (App. No. 3564/11), judgment of 28 May 2013; *Mudric v Moldova* (App. No. 74839/10), judgment of 16 July 2013; *T.M. and C.M. v Moldova* (App. No. 26608/11), judgment of 28 January 2014; *M.G. v Turkey* (App. No. 646/10) judgment of 22 March 2016; *Halime Kılıç v Turkey* (App. No. 63034/11), judgment of 28 June 2016. *Talpis v Italy* (App. No. 41237/14), judgment of 2 March 2017; *Balsan v Romania* (App. No. 49645/09), judgment of 23 May 2017; *Volodina v Russia* (App. No. 41261/17), judgment of 9 July 2019; *Tunikova and Others v Russia* (App. Nos. 55974/16, 53118/17, 27484/18, 28011/19), judgment of 14 December 2021; *Tkhelidze v Georgia* (App. No. 33056/17), judgment of 8 July 2021; *A and B v Georgia* (App. No. 73975/16), judgment of 10 February 2022; *A.E. v Bulgaria* (App. No. 53891/21), judgment of 23 May 2023; and *Luca v Moldova* (App. No. 55351/17), judgment of 17 October 2023.

49 (App. No. 33401/02), judgment of 9 September 2009. For further discussion of this case, see Burton, M., 'The Human Rights of Victims of Domestic Violence: *Opuz v Turkey*' (2010) 22 *Child and Family Law Quarterly* 131; and Londono, P., 'Developing Human Rights Principles in Cases of Gender-Based Violence: *Opuz v Turkey* in the European Court of Human Rights' (2009) 9 *Human Rights Law Review* 662.

50 At para. 200.

degrading treatment, or in some cases the right to life, may appear to be more apt. At the time of the drafting of CEDAW, violence against women was not generally viewed as a matter relating to gender-based discrimination as such, and it is therefore unsurprising that an instrument focused on eliminating such discrimination did not expressly encompass this issue.

The CEDAW Committee and Violence Against Women

Nevertheless, despite the omission from CEDAW of any express reference to violence against women, the CEDAW Committee has interpreted this instrument in such a way as to encompass this issue. Article 21 of CEDAW empowers the CEDAW Committee to make General Recommendations which are addressed to states parties generally and which usually explain the views of the Committee on the obligations contained in the Convention. In 1989 the CEDAW Committee issued its General Recommendation No. 12,[51] which related to violence against women. This Recommendation was however very brief and simply asserted that states parties should include, in their periodic reports to the Committee, information concerning the legislation in force to protect women against the incidence of all kinds of violence in everyday life, including sexual violence, abuses in the family and sexual harassment at the work place;[52] other measures adopted to eradicate this violence;[53] the existence of support services for women who were the victims of aggression or abuses;[54] and statistical data on the incidence of violence of all kinds against women and on women who are the victims of violence.[55] General Recommendation No. 12 did not explain though precisely how violence against women was encompassed by CEDAW.[56] It simply stated that Articles 2,[57] 5,[58] 11,[59] 12[60] and 16[61] of this instrument required states parties 'to act to protect women against violence of any kind occurring within the family, at the work place or in any other area of social life'. Nevertheless, given that none of these

51 Committee on the Elimination of Discrimination Against Women, U.N. Doc. A/44/38 (1989).
52 At para. 1.
53 At para. 2.
54 At para. 3.
55 At para. 4.
56 Šimonović, D., 'Global and Regional Standards on Violence Against Women: The Evolution and Synergy of the CEDAW and Istanbul Conventions' (2014) 36 *Human Rights Quarterly* 590 at 600.
57 Article 2 relates to policy measures.
58 Article 5 relates to stereotyping and prejudice.
59 Article 11 relates to employment.
60 Article 12 relates to health.
61 Article 16 relates to marriage and family life

provisions contain any express mention of violence against women, this statement was somewhat vague.

General Recommendation No. 12 was thus superseded three years later by General Recommendation No. 19,[62] which was a much more detailed document. This constituted an immensely important development as this General Recommendation officially interpreted CEDAW as prohibiting violence against women in both public and private contexts. As Chinkin comments, 'General Recommendation 19 has been the basis of the Committee's work on violence against women'.[63] General Recommendation No. 19 stated clearly, 'The full implementation of the Convention required States to take positive measures to eliminate all forms of violence against women'.[64] Chinkin remarks, 'General Recommendation 19 provides the first holistic international law definition of gender-based violence against women'.[65] The General Recommendation asserted,

> The definition of discrimination includes gender-based violence, that is, violence that is directed against a woman because she is a woman or that affects women disproportionately. It includes acts that inflict physical, mental or sexual harm or suffering, threats of such acts, coercion and other deprivations of liberty. Gender-based violence may breach specific provisions of the Convention, regardless of whether those provisions expressly mention violence.[66]

The General Recommendation stated that gender-based violence may breach *inter alia* the right to life; the right not to be subject to torture or to cruel, inhuman or degrading treatment or punishment; and the right to liberty and security of person.[67] It emphasised,

> that discrimination under the Convention is not restricted to action by or on behalf of Governments. . . . Under general international law and specific human rights covenants, States may be responsible for private acts if they fail to act with due diligence to prevent violations of rights or to investigate and punish acts of violence, and for providing compensation.[68]

62 Committee on the Elimination of Discrimination Against Women, U.N. Doc. A/47/38 (1992).
63 Chinkin and Freeman, op. cit. 473.
64 At para. 4.
65 Chinkin, C., 'Violence Against Women', in Freeman, M.A., Chinkin, C. and Rudolf, B. (eds.), *The UN Convention on the Elimination of All Forms of Discrimination Against Women – A Commentary*, 2012, Oxford University Press, Oxford, 443 at 452.
66 At para. 6.
67 At para. 7.
68 At para. 9.

In this way, the concept of state responsibility was used to great effect to transcend the public/private dichotomy. The General Recommendation also stated,

> Family violence is one of the most insidious forms of violence against women. It is prevalent in all societies. Within family relationships women of all ages are subjected to violence of all kinds, including battering, rape, other forms of sexual assault, mental and other forms of violence, which are perpetuated by traditional attitudes.[69]

The General Recommendation asserted that measures necessary to overcome family violence included 'criminal penalties where necessary', and that 'states parties should ensure that laws against family violence and abuse . . . give adequate protection to all women, and respect their integrity and dignity'.[70] The CEDAW Committee recognised that 'Effective legal measures, including . . . civil remedies'[71] were necessary to protect women from violence occurring in the private sphere. It has been argued that the provision of social support measures to victims of domestic abuse is the state response that is most needed by victims.[72] The necessity for such provision was recognised by the CEDAW Committee, and it was recommended that states parties provide 'Protective measures, including refuges, counselling, rehabilitation and support services for women who are the victims of violence or who are at risk of violence'.[73] The Committee also recommended that states provide public education programmes to change attitudes concerning the status of men and women,[74] and stated that gender-sensitive training of judicial and law enforcement officers and other public officials was essential for the effective implementation of the Convention.[75] In addition, the Committee recommended that states parties provide rehabilitation programmes for perpetrators,[76] and asserted that they 'should encourage the compilation of statistics and research on the extent, causes and effects of violence, and on the effectiveness of measures to prevent and deal with violence'.[77]

69 At para. 23.
70 At para. 24.
71 At para. 24.
72 Schneider, E., *Battered Women & Feminist Lawmaking*, 2000, Yale University Press, Connecticut, 196–197.
73 At para. 24(t)(iii).
74 At para. 24(t)(ii).
75 At para. 24(b).
76 At para. 24(r)(iv).
77 At para. 24(c).

In 2017, the CEDAW Committee then adopted its General Recommendation No. 35 on gender-based violence against women.[78] The purpose of this General Recommendation was to update General Recommendation No. 19, which was by then 25 years old. In General Recommendation No. 35, the CEDAW Committee pointed out that, despite the work of the Committee and of other bodies such as civil society groups, 'gender-based violence against women . . . remains pervasive in all countries of the world, with high levels of impunity'.[79] The aim of the CEDAW Committee in adopting General Recommendation No. 35 was to provide states parties with 'further guidance aimed at accelerating the elimination of gender-based violence against women'.[80]

In General Recommendation No. 19, the CEDAW Committee made the point that 'Gender-based violence may breach specific provisions of the Convention, regardless of whether those provisions expressly mention violence'.[81] However, General Recommendation No. 35 went considerably further and stated, 'Gender-based violence against women constitutes discrimination against women under Article 1 and therefore engages all of the obligations in the Convention'.[82] Whilst a large part of General Recommendation No. 19 was devoted to a section entitled 'Comments on specific articles of the Convention', which explained how a selection of provisions of CEDAW related to violence against women, a different approach was adopted in General Recommendation No. 35. Although specific provisions of CEDAW were referred to in the latter, overall there was less of an emphasis on explaining how precisely the specific provisions of CEDAW mandate the obligations and recommendations put forward by the CEDAW Committee. Nevertheless, General Recommendations No. 35 provided substantially more detail on the Committee's views on the responsibilities of states parties in relation to addressing the issue of violence against women. General Recommendation No. 35 will be analysed further in Chapter Four.

Using the interpretation of CEDAW put forward in General Recommendation No. 19 and then in General Recommendation No. 35, the CEDAW Committee frequently makes recommendations relating to violence against

78 Committee on the Elimination of Discrimination Against Women, CEDAW/C/GC/35 (2017).

79 At para. 6.

80 At para. 3.

81 At para. 6.

82 At para. 21. Article 1 of CEDAW states, 'For the purposes of the present Convention, the term "discrimination against women" shall mean any distinction, exclusion or restriction made on the basis of sex which has the effect or purpose of impairing or nullifying the recognition, enjoyment or exercise by women, irrespective of their marital status, on a basis of equality of men and women, of human rights and fundamental freedoms in the political, economic, social, cultural, civil or any other field'.

women in its Concluding Observations on the reports submitted by states under CEDAW's monitoring procedure.[83]

In addition, under the individual communications procedure found in the Optional Protocol to CEDAW, the Committee has found states to be in breach of the Convention in situations relating to violence against women and has in these instances made recommendations as to how the states in question should respond to these findings and rectify the situations in question.[84] The Optional Protocol to CEDAW, which entered into force in December 2000, allows individuals or groups to submit claims of violations of the Convention to the CEDAW Committee. Communications may also be submitted on behalf of individuals with their consent, unless acting on their behalf without their consent may be justified. Under Article 4 of the Optional Protocol, the CEDAW Committee may only consider a communication if all domestic remedies have been exhausted, or if the application of such remedies would be unnecessarily prolonged or unlikely to bring relief to the complainant. A communication is inadmissible if the same matter has already been examined by the CEDAW Committee or has been considered by another international procedure. A communication is also inadmissible if it is incompatible with CEDAW, manifestly ill-founded, an abuse of the right to petition, or if the subject of the communication occurred prior to the entry into force of the Optional Protocol for the state in question. Under Article 5, the CEDAW Committee may recommend interim measures to the state party at any time between the receipt of a communication and its decision. Under Article 7, when a communication is submitted, the Committee should bring it to the attention of the state in question. The state then has six months to submit an explanation to the Committee. Communications are considered by the Committee in closed meetings. The views of the Committee are then transmitted to the parties. The state is required to respond in writing within six months, including a description of any action which it has taken on the matter. The Preamble to the Optional Protocol asserts that it is a reaffirmation of the determination of states parties 'to ensure the full and equal enjoyment by women of all human rights and fundamental freedoms and to take effective action to prevent violations of these rights and freedoms'. Essentially the Protocol gives to every woman in states which have ratified it an opportunity to go to the CEDAW Committee and argue that the state has failed to protect her rights under the Convention.

83 For example, see paras. 29–30 of the Concluding Observations of the CEDAW Committee on the eighth periodic report of the United Kingdom, 14 March 2019, CEDAW/C/GBR/CO/8.

84 See for example, *AT v Hungary* (Communication No.: 2/2003, 26 January 2005, CEDAW/C/32/D/2/2003); *Goekce v Austria* (Communication No.: 5/2005, 6 August 2007, CEDAW/C/39/D/5/2005); *Yildirim v Austria* (Communication No.: 6/2005, 1 October 2007, CEDAW/C/39/D/6/2005); *VK v Bulgaria* (Communication No.: 20/2008, 17 August 2011, CEDAW/C/49/D/20/2008); *Jallow v Bulgaria* (Communication No.: 32/2011, 28 August 2012, CEDAW/C/52/D/32/2011).

AT v Hungary[85] was the first decision of the CEDAW Committee on the merits of a communication under the Optional Protocol. The views of the Committee were adopted on 26 January 2005. In this case the complainant alleged that for the past four years she had been subjected to domestic abuse and serious threats by her partner. The couple had two children, one of whom suffered from severe brain damage. The perpetrator was in possession of a firearm and had threatened to kill the complainant, however the latter had been unable to go to a shelter, as there were no shelters which were equipped to take in the disabled child, together with his mother and sister. There were also no protection orders or restraining orders available under Hungarian law. Although the perpetrator eventually moved out of the family apartment, his subsequent visits involved more incidents of violence, which were aggravated by him being in a drunken state. When he left the family home, he took most of the furniture and household items with him, and he did not pay child support for three years. The complainant alleged that the state had violated her rights under Article 2 of CEDAW, under which states parties agree to 'pursue by all appropriate means and without delay a policy of eliminating discrimination against women' and, to this end, undertake 'to embody the principle of the equality of men and women in their national constitutions or other appropriate legislation if not yet incorporated therein and to ensure, through law and other appropriate means, the practical realization of this principle';[86] 'to adopt appropriate legislative and other measures, including sanctions where appropriate, prohibiting all discrimination against women';[87] and 'to take all appropriate measures to eliminate discrimination against women by any person, organization or enterprise'.[88] In addition, the complainant alleged that the state had violated Article 5(a) of CEDAW, under which,

> States Parties shall take all appropriate measures to modify the social and cultural patterns of conduct of men and women, with a view to achieving the elimination of prejudices and customary and all other practices which are based on the idea of the inferiority or the superiority of either of the sexes or on stereotyped roles for men and women.

The complainant also alleged that there had been a breach of Article 16 under which 'States Parties shall take all appropriate measures to eliminate discrimination against women in all matters relating to marriage and family relations'.

In examining the complaint, the CEDAW Committee stated that the obligations contained in Article 2(a), (b) and (e) of the Convention 'extend to the

85 Communication No. 2/2003, views adopted 26 January 2005, CEDAW/C/32/D/2/2003.

86 Article 2(a).

87 Article 2(b).

88 Article 2(e).

prevention of and protection from violence against women, which obligations in the present case, remain unfulfilled and constitute a violation of the (complainant's) human rights and fundamental freedoms, particularly her right to security of person'.[89] In relation to Articles 5(a) and 16 of the Convention, the Committee noted, 'traditional attitudes by which women are regarded as subordinate to men contribute to violence against them'.[90] In applying this principle to the situation in question, the Committee stated,

> For four years and continuing to the present day, the [complainant] has felt threatened by her former common law husband, the father of her two children. The [complainant] has been battered by this same man, her former common law husband. She has been unsuccessful, either through civil or criminal proceedings, to temporarily or permanently bar [him] from the apartment where she and her children have continued to reside. The [complainant] could not have asked for a restraining or protection order since neither option currently exists in the State party. She has been unable to flee to a shelter because none are equipped to accept her together with her children, one of whom is fully disabled.[91]

The Committee therefore proceeded to find the state party to be in violation of Articles 2(a), (b) and (e), 5(a) and 16 of CEDAW.

In relation to the complainant herself, the Committee recommended that the state adopt immediate measures to guarantee her physical and mental integrity and that of her family. She should also be given a safe home in which to live with her children, appropriate child support and legal assistance, and reparation proportionate to the physical and mental harm which she had suffered and to the seriousness of the breach of her rights. At a more general level, the Committee recommended *inter alia* that the state 'Respect, protect, promote and fulfil women's human rights, including their right to be free from all forms of domestic violence, including intimidation and threats of torture', and that the state should 'Assure victims of domestic violence the maximum protection of the law by acting with due diligence to prevent and respond to such violence against women'.[92] The Committee also recommended that the state adopt all necessary measures to provide regular training on CEDAW and the Optional Protocol thereto to judges, lawyers and law enforcement officials. The state should introduce a specific law prohibiting domestic violence against women and providing for protection and exclusion orders as well as support services, including shelters, and should 'Investigate promptly,

89 At para. 9.3.
90 At para. 9.4.
91 At para. 9.4.
92 At para. 9.6.

thoroughly, impartially and seriously all allegations of domestic violence and bring the offenders to justice in accordance with international standards'.[93] In addition, victims of domestic violence should be provided with 'safe and prompt access to justice, including free legal aid where necessary, in order to ensure them available, effective and sufficient remedies and rehabilitation'.[94] The Committee also recommended that the state provide offenders with rehabilitation programmes, and programmes on non-violent conflict resolution methods.

It is worth noting that the decision in *AT v Hungary* demonstrates the fact that the CEDAW Committee has adopted a flexible approach to the admissibility requirements under the Optional Protocol. As stated earlier, under Article 4 of the Protocol, the CEDAW Committee may only consider a communication if all domestic remedies have been exhausted, or if the application of such remedies would be unnecessarily prolonged or unlikely to bring relief to the complainant. In this instance, there were domestic civil proceedings pending as regards the perpetrator's access to the apartment, but the Committee recognised that these proceedings were unlikely to result in effective relief. Criminal proceedings had also been initiated, but these proceedings had been delayed for more than three years and in the opinion of the Committee this constituted an 'unreasonable prolonged delay' for the purposes of Article 4 of the Optional Protocol. Also, even though the majority of the violence in this case had in fact taken place prior to the entry into force of the Optional Protocol in Hungary, the Committee nevertheless was of the view that in examining the complaint the inaction of the state as regards all of the violence should be considered.[95]

In August 2007 the CEDAW Committee examined two more communications surrounding the issue of domestic abuse. *Goekce v Austria*[96] concerned a victim of domestic abuse who had eventually been killed by her husband. The communication was brought by the Vienna Intervention Centre Against Domestic Violence and the Association for Women's Access to Justice, on behalf of the family members of the deceased. In examining the complaint the Committee noted that the state had established a comprehensive model to address domestic abuse which encompassed legislation, criminal and civil law remedies, awareness-raising measures, education and training, the provision

93 At para. 9.6.
94 At para. 9.6.
95 Chinkin, 'Violence Against Women', 456.
96 Communication No. 5/2005, views adopted 6 August 2007, CEDAW/C/39/D/5/2005.

of shelters, counselling for victims and work with perpetrators. However, the Committee then stated,

> in order for the individual woman victim of domestic violence to enjoy the practical realization of the principle of equality of men and women and of her human rights and fundamental freedoms, the political will that is expressed in the aforementioned comprehensive system of Austria must be supported by State actors, who adhere to the State party's due diligence obligations.[97]

The Committee noted that the police had been called frequently during the three-year period prior to the homicide, in relation to disturbances, disputes and incidents of battering. The police had issued prohibition to return orders to the perpetrator on three occasions, and had twice requested, without success, that the Public Prosecutor order that the perpetrator be detained. Indeed, a three-month interim injunction had been in effect at the time of the victim's death which prohibited the perpetrator from returning to the family apartment and its immediate environs and from contacting the victim or their children. The Committee also noted that although the victim had called the emergency call service a few hours before she had been killed, no police patrol car had been sent to the scene of the crime. In the view of the Committee, due to this combination of factors, the police either knew or should have known that the victim was in serious danger and should therefore have treated the last call from her as an emergency. The police were thus accountable for failing to exercise due diligence in protecting the victim. In addition, the Committee stated that the Public Prosecutor should not have denied the requests which had been made by the police to arrest and detain the perpetrator.

The Committee therefore held that the state had violated its obligations under Article 2(a) of CEDAW. The state had also breached its duties under Article 2(c), (d), (e) and (f), namely that it should 'establish legal protection of the rights of women on an equal basis with men and . . . ensure through competent national tribunals and other public institutions the effective protection of women against any act of discrimination';[98] 'refrain from engaging in any act or practice of discrimination against women and . . . ensure that public authorities and institutions shall act in conformity with this obligation';[99] 'take all appropriate measures to eliminate discrimination against women by any person, organization or enterprise;[100] and 'take all appropriate measures, including legislation, to modify or abolish existing laws, regulations, customs

97 At para. 12.1.2.
98 Article 2(c).
99 Article 2(d).
100 Article 2(e).

and practices which constitute discrimination against women'.[101] In addition, the state had violated its obligations under Article 3 of the Convention, under which states must take all appropriate measures 'to ensure the full development and advancement of women, for the purpose of guaranteeing them the exercise and enjoyment of human rights and fundamental freedoms on a basis of equality with men', when taken in conjunction with the definition of 'discrimination against women' found in Article 1 and with General Recommendation No. 19.

The Committee therefore recommended that the state act with due diligence to prevent and respond to violence against women and provide for adequate sanctions for the failure to do so. The state should also

> Vigilantly and in a speedy manner prosecute perpetrators of domestic violence in order to convey to the offenders and to the public that society condemns domestic violence as well as ensure that criminal and civil measures are utilized in cases where the perpetrator in a domestic violence situation poses a dangerous threat to the victim; and also ensure that in all action taken to protect women from violence, due consideration is given to the safety of women, emphasizing that the perpetrator's rights cannot supersede women's human rights to life and to physical and mental integrity.[102]

In addition, the state should ensure enhanced coordination among law enforcement and judicial officers and strengthen training programmes on domestic abuse for judges, lawyers and law enforcement officials, including on CEDAW, the Optional Protocol thereto and General Recommendation No. 19. It was also recommended that the state ensure that 'all levels of the criminal justice system (police, public prosecutors, judges) routinely cooperate with non-governmental organizations that work to protect and support women victims of gender-based violence'.[103]

Yildirim v Austria[104] likewise concerned a victim of domestic abuse who had eventually been killed by her husband. Again the communication was brought by the Vienna Intervention Centre Against Domestic Violence and the Association for Women's Access to Justice, on behalf of the family members of the deceased. In this instance, the victim had been in ongoing contact with the police and had authorised the prosecution of her husband. The police had made requests to the Public Prosecutor for the arrest and detention of the perpetrator, however these requests had been denied. The perpetrator had made continuous efforts to contact the victim and had threatened by phone

101 Article 2(f).
102 At para. 12.3(b).
103 At para. 12.3(c).
104 Communication No. 6/2005, views adopted 6 August 2007, CEDAW/C/39/D/6/2005.

and in person to kill her, despite the existence of an interim injunction which prohibited him from returning to the couple's apartment, the immediate surroundings and the victim's workplace, as well as from contacting the victim. The CEDAW Committee stated that the facts disclosed a situation which was extremely dangerous to the victim of which the state authorities knew or ought to have known, and as such the Public Prosecutor should not have denied the requests of the police to arrest the perpetrator and place him in detention. Indeed, the Public Prosecutor's denial of these requests constituted a violation of the state's due diligence obligation to protect the victim. Again the Committee emphasised that 'the perpetrator's rights cannot supersede women's human rights to life and to physical and mental integrity'.[105] As in *Goekce v Austria*, the Committee found violations of Articles 2(a), 2(c) through (f), and 3 of CEDAW, read in conjunction with Article 1 and General Recommendation No. 19. The recommendations which had been made to the state in *Goekce v Austria* were then reiterated.

The approaches adopted by the CEDAW Committee in examining the complaints in *Goekce v Austria* and *Yildirim v Austria* were certainly very positive. Nevertheless, it has been commented that the Committee could actually have taken an even stronger approach. For instance, Chinkin notes that in examining these cases the Committee did not state that even the extreme forms of domestic abuse, which had occurred in these instances and which had indeed resulted in the deaths of the victims, amounted to torture.[106]

Another communication relating to domestic abuse was considered by the CEDAW Committee on 27 September 2011. In *V.K. v Bulgaria*[107] the complainant alleged that the state had failed to provide her with effective protection against abuse on the part of her husband. The complainant had been subjected to psychological, emotional and economic abuse, and later also to physical violence. Her husband had not permitted her to work, despite her education and qualifications. The complainant was entirely dependent economically on her husband, who alone decided on the spending of the family's income and who provided the complainant with money only for the basic needs of the family. In addition, the complainant was not permitted to communicate freely with friends and family members. The complainant's attempts to discuss the situation with her husband resulted in conflicts and in physical

105 At para. 12.1.5.

106 Chinkin, op. cit. 473. Various academic commentators have likened domestic abuse to torture, for example, Copelon, R., 'Intimate Terror: Understanding Domestic Violence as Torture', in Cook, R.J. (ed.), *Human Rights of Women – National and International Perspectives*, 1994, University of Pennsylvania Press, Philadelphia, 116; and Grdinic, E., 'Application of the Elements of Torture and Other Forms of Ill-Treatment, as Defined by the European Court and Commission of Human Rights, to the Incidents of Domestic Violence' (2000) 23 *Hastings International and Comparative Law Review* 217.

107 Communication No. 20/2008, views adopted 27 September 2011, CEDAW/C/49/D/20/2008.

violence. In considering the complaint, the Committee noted that the state had adopted legislation against domestic abuse, which encompassed a fast-track procedure for issuing immediate protection orders. However, a permanent protection order had not been issued against the complainant's husband, and in addition no shelter provision had been available. The Committee stated that in order for the complainant

> to enjoy the practical realization of the principle of equality between women and men and of her human rights and fundamental freedoms, the political will that is expressed in such specific legislation must be supported by all State actors, including the courts, which are bound by the obligations of the State party.[108]

The Committee was of the view that in refusing to issue a permanent protection order, the national courts had applied 'an overly restrictive definition of domestic violence'[109] which was not warranted by the domestic legislation. The courts had 'focused exclusively on the issue of direct and immediate threat to the life or health of the (complainant) and on her physical integrity, while neglecting her emotional and psychological suffering'.[110] According to the Committee, such an approach reflected 'a stereotyped and overly narrow concept of what constitutes domestic violence',[111] and the refusal of the domestic courts to issue a permanent protection order against the complainant's husband was therefore based on 'preconceived and thus discriminatory notions of what constitutes domestic violence'.[112] The comments of the Committee serve to emphasise the importance of recognising psychological and economic aspects of domestic abuse. The CEDAW Committee was also of the view that the unavailability of shelters constituted a breach of the state's obligations under Article 2(c) and (e) of the Convention to provide for the immediate protection of women from violence, including from domestic abuse. Overall, the Committee found that the state had failed to fulfil its obligations under Article 2(c), (d), (e) and (f), in conjunction with Article 1; and Article 5(a), in conjunction with Article 16, as well as with General Recommendation No. 19.

The Committee proceeded to recommend that the state provide adequate financial compensation to the complainant commensurate with the gravity of the violation of her rights. At a more general level, the Committee recommended *inter alia* that the state amend the national legislation on

108 At para. 9.4.
109 At para. 9.9.
110 At para. 9.9.
111 At para. 9.12.
112 At para. 9.12.

domestic abuse to ensure that protection orders are available without placing undue administrative and legal burdens on applicants. The state should also ensure that a sufficient number of state-funded shelters are available to victims of domestic abuse and their children and provide support to non-governmental organisations which offer shelter and other means of support to victims of domestic abuse. In addition, the state should provide mandatory training for judges, lawyers and law enforcement personnel on the application of the national domestic violence legislation, including on the definition of domestic abuse and on gender stereotypes, as well as appropriate training on CEDAW, the Optional Protocol thereto, and the Committee's General Recommendations, in particular General Recommendation No. 19.

Another communication concerning Bulgaria's response to the issue of domestic abuse was considered by the CEDAW Committee on 23 July 2012. *Jallow v Bulgaria*[113] involved a situation wherein both parties to a relationship had made allegations of domestic abuse, however the complainant, who was a Gambian national, argued that the state had not provided her with the same protection as had been afforded to her husband. The complainant was a Gambian national who was illiterate and who spoke only her native language and English at an average level. The Committee commented,

> In contrast with her husband's application under the [national domestic violence legislation] that was duly heard, the State party's authorities failed to act with due diligence, to provide her with effective protection and to take into account her vulnerable position, as an illiterate migrant woman with a small daughter without a command of Bulgarian or relatives in the State party.[114]

In considering the complaint, the Committee stated, 'traditional attitudes by which women are regarded as subordinate to men contribute to violence against them'.[115] The Committee noted that in the case in question, the state authorities had relied on the husband's statement and actions, despite being aware of the complainant's vulnerable position and her dependency on him. The Committee commented, 'the authorities based their activities on a stereotyped notion that the husband was superior and that his opinions should be taken seriously, disregarding the fact that domestic violence proportionately affects women considerably more than men'.[116] Due to an emergency protection order which had been issued in favour of the complainant's husband, the

113 Communication No. 32/2011, views adopted 23 July 2012, CEDAW/C/52/D/32/2011.
114 At para. 8.2.
115 At para. 8.6.
116 At para. 8.6.

complainant had been separated from her daughter for almost eight months, during which time she had received no information regarding the care which her daughter was receiving and had been granted no visitation rights. The Committee considered therefore that both the complainant and her daughter were victims of gender-based discrimination because the state had failed to protect the complainant's equal rights in marriage and as a parent and had failed to regard her daughter's interests as being paramount. The emergency protection order had been issued without due consideration having been taken of the complainant's claim that she and her daughter were in fact the ones who were in need of protection from domestic abuse.

The Committee was thus of the view that the state had failed to fulfil its obligations under Article 2(b), (c), (d), (e) and (f) and Article 5(a) of CEDAW. In addition, the state had failed to fulfil its duties under Article 16(c), (d) and (f), namely to ensure, on a basis of equality of men and women, '(t)he same rights and responsibilities during marriage and at its dissolution';[117] '(t)he same rights and responsibilities as parents, irrespective of their marital status, in matters relating to their children';[118] and '(t)he same rights and responsibilities with regard to guardianship, wardship, trusteeship and adoption of children, or similar institutions where these concepts exist in national legislation'.[119] Article 16(d) and (f) also state, 'in all cases the interests of the children shall be paramount'.

The Committee therefore recommended that the state provide the complainant and her daughter with appropriate compensation commensurate with the gravity of the violation of their rights. At a more general level, the Committee asserted that the state should

> take measures to ensure that women victims of domestic violence, in particular migrant women, have effective access to services related to protection against domestic violence and to justice, including interpretation or translation of documents, and that the manner in which domestic courts apply the law is consistent with the State party's obligations under the Convention.[120]

The state should also 'take the legislative or other measures necessary to ensure that, in the determination of custody and visitation rights of children,

117 CEDAW, Article 16(c).
118 Article 16(d).
119 Article 16(f).
120 At para. 8.8.

incidents of violence are taken into account and that the rights and safety of the victim or children are not jeopardized'.[121] In addition, the state should

> Provide for appropriate and regular training on the Convention, its Optional Protocol and its general recommendations for judges, prosecutors . . . and law enforcement personnel in a gender-sensitive manner, having particular regard to multiple discrimination, so as to ensure that complaints regarding gender-based violence are received and considered adequately.[122]

As can be seen from its response to these communications under the Optional Protocol procedure, the CEDAW Committee works very much from the assumption that, given the interpretations put forward in General Recommendation Nos. 19 and 35, CEDAW without doubt applies to violence against women.

Other UN Bodies and Violence Against Women

In addition, it is notable that consideration of the issue of violence against women is not limited only to the CEDAW Committee. It is undoubtedly the case that a substantial amount of activity has already taken place, and continues to occur, at the UN level on violence against women. This issue was addressed in the Vienna Declaration and Programme of Action which was adopted by the World Conference on Human Rights in Vienna in 1993.[123] Following this event, a Special Rapporteur on violence against women, its causes and consequences, was appointed by the UN Commission on Human Rights. The Special Rapporteur's mandate is to

> seek and receive information on violence against women, its causes and consequences, from Governments, treaty bodies, specialized agencies, other special rapporteurs . . . [and] recommend measures, ways and means, at the national, regional and international level to eliminate violence against women and its causes, and to remedy its consequences.[124]

It has been remarked that the Special Rapporteur on violence against women has 'brought international consciousness to a new level'.[125] Since the inception

121 At para. 8.8.

122 At para. 8.8.

123 The Vienna Declaration and Programme of Action can be found at http://www.ohchr.org/EN/ProfessionalInterest/Pages/Vienna.aspx, Office of the High Commissioner for Human Rights.

124 U.N. Commission on Human Rights, Resolution 1994/45, paras. 7(a) and (b).

125 Stark, B., 'Symposium on Integrating Responses to Domestic Violence' (2001) 47 *Loyola Law Review* 255 at 265.

of this post, those who have held the office have issued a multitude of detailed reports.

The UN General Assembly has also made recommendations relating to states' responses to violence against women. For example, even as far back as 1985, the General Assembly urged member states to take action 'in order to prevent domestic violence and to render the appropriate assistance to the victims thereof';[126] to adopt specific measures with a view to making criminal and civil justice systems more sensitive in responding to domestic violence;[127] and to ensure coordination of social welfare and criminal justice measures in relation to such abuse.[128] In 1990 the General Assembly again urged states

> to begin or continue to explore, develop and implement multidisciplinary policies, measures and strategies, within and outside of the criminal justice system, with respect to domestic violence in all its facets, including legal, law enforcement, judicial, societal, educational, psychological, economic, health-related and correctional aspects.[129]

In 1993 the General Assembly issued its important Declaration on the Elimination of Violence Against Women, which referred to the rights to life; to equality; to liberty and security of person; to equal protection under the law; to be free from all forms of discrimination; to the highest standard attainable of physical and mental health; to just and favourable conditions of work; and not to be subjected to torture, or other cruel, inhuman or degrading treatment or punishment.[130] As a General Assembly Resolution, the Declaration is not a legally binding instrument, however, 'The fact that the Resolution was adopted without a vote, but by consensus amongst States, has added to its weight and authority'.[131] In this Declaration, the General Assembly asserted that states 'should pursue by all appropriate means and without delay a policy of eliminating violence against women'.[132] For example, they should 'Develop penal, civil, labour and administrative sanctions in domestic legislation to punish and redress the wrongs caused to women who are subjected to violence'.[133]

126 General Assembly Resolution 40/36 (1985) at para. 2.

127 At para. 7.

128 At para. 7(j).

129 General Assembly Resolution 45/114 (1990) at para. 1.

130 General Assembly Resolution A/RES/48/104, 20 December 1993, Article 3. See also for example, the Resolutions of the General Assembly on intensification of efforts to eliminate all forms of violence against women which were adopted on 19 December 2006 (A/RES/61/143); 18 December 2007 (A/RES/62/133); 18 December 2008 (A/RES/63/155); 18 December 2009 (A/RES/64/137); 21 December 2010 (A/RES/65/187); 20 December 2012 (A/RES/67/144).

131 Rehman, op. cit., 552.

132 General Assembly Resolution 48/104 (1993), Article 4.

133 Article 4(d).

States should also 'Develop, in a comprehensive way, preventive approaches and all those measures of a legal, political, administrative and cultural nature that promote the protection of women against any form of violence'.[134] States were urged to

> Work to ensure, to the maximum extent feasible in the light of their available resources and, where needed, within the framework of international cooperation, that women subjected to violence and, where appropriate, their children have specialized assistance, such as rehabilitation, assistance in child care and maintenance, treatment, counselling, and health and social services, facilities and programmes, as well as support structures, and should take all other appropriate measures to promote their safety and physical and psychological rehabilitation.[135]

The Declaration also urged states to 'Consider the possibility of developing national plans of action to promote the protection of women against any form of violence . . . taking into account . . . such cooperation as can be provided by non-governmental organizations'.[136] As Rehman comments, the Declaration 'has had a considerable impact in developing the law relating to women's rights and has provided substantial ammunition to CEDAW to scrutinise practices which contravene the provisions of the Declaration'.[137]

The Fourth World Conference on Women was held in 1995 in Beijing. The Beijing Platform for Action urged states to adopt a wide range of measures regarding violence against women, and asserted that states should,

> Provide women who are subjected to violence with access to the mechanisms of justice and, as provided for by national legislation, to just and effective remedies for the harm they have suffered and inform women of their rights in seeking redress through such mechanisms.[138]

The Platform for Action emphasised that governments should support initiatives of women's organisations to raise awareness of the issue of violence against women[139] and that they should organise and fund community-based campaigns to raise awareness about violence against women as a human rights violation.[140] States should also 'Provide well-funded shelters and relief support for girls and women subjected to violence, as well as medical,

134 Article 4(f).
135 Article 4(g).
136 Article 4(e).
137 Rehman, op. cit., 552.
138 Beijing Platform for Action, U.N. Doc. A/CONF. 177/20 (1995), at para. 124(b).
139 At para. 125(d).
140 At para. 125(e).

psychological and other counselling services and free or low-cost legal aid, where it is needed, as well as appropriate assistance to enable them to find a means of subsistence'.[141]

In addition, the UN Commission on Human Rights also issued statements relevant to violence against women. For example, in 2001 the Commission on Human Rights issued a Resolution on the elimination of violence against women in which it called upon states *inter alia* to condemn violence against women;[142] to take action to investigate and punish persons who perpetrate acts of violence against women;[143] to support initiatives undertaken by women's organisations and non-governmental organisations on the elimination of violence against women;[144] and to consider undertaking campaigns about violence against women.[145] Similar statements were also made by the Commission in a 2004 Resolution on the elimination of violence against women.[146] In 2006, the Commission on Human Rights was superseded by the Human Rights Council,[147] and in 2010 the latter issued a Resolution on 'accelerating efforts to eliminate all forms of violence against women' which again urged states to adopt a range of measures as regards this issue.[148] A further Resolution on violence against women was issued by the Human Rights Council in 2012.[149]

Conclusion

As was discussed in this chapter, none of the UN human rights treaties refer expressly to violence against women, and there are no legally binding treaty provisions at the global level which address this issue. Potential reasons for the omission from CEDAW of specific reference to violence against women include the fact that this instrument was adopted 45 years ago, at a time when there was less understanding of the importance and prevalence of such violence. Also, human rights were originally formulated in such a manner as to create a 'public/private divide', whereby rights were deemed to be applicable in the 'public' sphere where the state was directly involved, but were not deemed to apply in the 'private' sphere in situations involving only

141 At para. 125(a).

142 Commission on Human Rights Resolution 2001/49, at para. 9(b).

143 At para. 10(c).

144 At para. 10(d).

145 At para. 10(e).

146 Commission on Human Rights Resolution 2004/46, at para. 15(j).

147 Pursuant to General Assembly Resolution 60/251 of 15 March 2006, all mandates, mechanisms, functions and responsibilities of the Commission on Human Rights were assumed, as of 19 June 2006, by the Human Rights Council.

148 Human Rights Council Resolution 14/12, 30 June 2010.

149 Human Rights Council Resolution 20/12, 5 July 2012.

private individuals. As the majority of violence against women occurs in the 'private' sphere, the existence of the public/private dichotomy meant that such violence was largely excluded from the rights discourse. In addition, it must be remembered that technically the aim of CEDAW was to combat discrimination against women, as opposed to securing the rights of women more substantively. At the time of the drafting of CEDAW, violence against women was not generally viewed as a matter relating to gender-based discrimination as such.

Nevertheless, despite the omission from CEDAW of any express reference to violence against women, the CEDAW Committee has interpreted this instrument in such a way as to encompass this issue, and other UN bodies have also addressed the subject of violence against women. Given the extensive consideration of violence against women which is afforded by the CEDAW Committee and also other UN bodies, the question arises of whether reform of the international legal framework on violence against women is really needed. Chapter Three will therefore consider the reasons why the lack of legally binding provisions on violence against women is problematic.

3 Why the Lack of Legally Binding Provisions on Violence Against Women Is Problematic

Chapter Three examines why reform of the international legal framework on violence against women is needed.[1] Although a multitude of statements have been issued by the CEDAW Committee and by other UN bodies on this issue, these all fall within the category of 'soft law', which is non-binding on states. This situation is potentially problematic from two perspectives. The first of these relates to whether is it acceptable from the perspective of principle that there are still no legally binding standards at the global level on the issue of violence against women. The second, and arguably even more crucial, aspect is more pragmatic in nature and centres on the argument that the absence of legally binding provisions at the global level on violence against women makes states less responsive to the need to adopt meaningful and effective measures in this area.

As regards the first aspect, the chapter argues that it is unacceptable from the perspective of principle that there are no legally binding provisions on violence against women at the global level. When CEDAW was adopted in 1979, the prevalence and nature of violence against women was not understood to any great extent. However, since then there have been enormous developments in the understanding of this phenomenon, and it is now no longer tenable for the lack of UN treaty provisions on violence against women to remain unaddressed. Such provisions would have a symbolic value, demonstrating the importance of the issue of such violence. At present it appears that one almost has to twist CEDAW in order to attempt to make this instrument encompass the issue of violence against women, and the adoption of legally binding provisions at the global level would add substantially more force to the statements made by the CEDAW Committee and the other UN human rights bodies as regards this issue.

In addition, the chapter considers whether the lack of legally binding provisions at the UN level on violence against women is also problematic from

1 See also McQuigg, R., 'Is It Time for a UN Treaty on Violence Against Women?' (2018) 22 *International Journal of Human Rights* 305.

DOI: 10.4324/9781003603689-3

a practical perspective. This involves discussion of two inter-related issues. These are, firstly, whether the existence of human rights standards actually makes a difference as regards the responses of states to particular issues; and secondly, if so, whether it matters in terms of state responses whether the human rights standards in question are legally binding or otherwise. Although there are of course considerable difficulties with the implementation of human rights standards, it is argued that the existence of such standards do make a significant difference regarding how states respond to particular issues. It is also argued that human rights standards need to be legally binding in order for them to attain a sufficient degree of efficacy. Additionally, the chapter argues that the fact that there are a number of legally binding provisions on violence against women within the context of regional systems of human rights protection by no means eliminates the need for legally binding provisions at the UN level on this issue.

Are There Advantages to the Current System?

It may be argued that there could be certain, albeit limited, advantages to a system whereby non-binding General Recommendations issued by an UN body are used to bring an issue within the ambit of international human rights norms, as opposed to having legally binding treaty provisions on the issue in question. For example, it is not disputed that the CEDAW Committee's General Recommendation No. 35[2] (the content of which will be discussed further in Chapter Four) consists largely of very positive measures which, if implemented by all states, may well result in a substantial reduction in the prevalence of violence against women. The use of a non-binding General Recommendation, as opposed to a treaty, could be said to allow for much greater flexibility in terms of what can be included. In order for states to be subject to a treaty, they must firstly sign and ratify the instrument in question. Essentially a state can only be subject to a treaty provision to which it has agreed. If a state wishes to become party to a treaty, but objects to a particular provision, it may be possible for the state to enter a reservation to that provision. If this is not permissible, the state must choose whether it still wishes to go ahead and ratify the treaty or if its objection to the provision in question is strong enough to preclude ratification. Either way, a state only becomes party to a treaty if it agrees (reluctantly or otherwise) to the provisions contained therein. Indeed in order for a treaty to enter into force at all, a certain number of ratifications by states will be needed.

2 Committee on the Elimination of Discrimination Against Women, General Recommendation No. 35 on gender-based violence against women, updating General Recommendation No. 19, CEDAW/C/GC/35 (2017).

Conversely, a General Recommendation can be issued by the CEDAW Committee without securing the agreement of any state as regards the content. Essentially the Committee can include whatever content it sees fit and then refer to this content in documents such as Concluding Observations on the periodic reports submitted by states parties to CEDAW and in its decisions on communications submitted under the individual complaints procedure. The content of the General Recommendation can also be used by civil society groups in campaigning. It is therefore the case that if a state is party to CEDAW, it may find that the CEDAW Committee refers to content which, although found in a General Recommendation, the state in question would not have signed up to had such provisions been contained in a treaty. The state may also find itself under pressure from civil society groups to comply with the measures in question. However, with a treaty, there is less flexibility in terms of what can be included.[3] If the content of a treaty is not acceptable to a state, it simply will not become party to that treaty, and will not therefore come within the 'jurisdiction' of the relevant treaty monitoring body. Although pressure can certainly be placed upon a state to ratify a treaty, it cannot be criticised as such for failing to implement the measures contained in a treaty which it has not ratified. By contrast, states frequently face criticism from the CEDAW Committee for failing to implement measures which, although not referred to expressly by CEDAW, have been recommended by the Committee in documents such as General Recommendation No. 35.

Problems of Principle

Nevertheless, there are also very considerable difficulties involved with reliance on a non-binding interpretation of CEDAW, as opposed to legally binding treaty provisions. Even though a multitude of statements have been issued by the CEDAW Committee and by other UN bodies, these all fall within the category of 'soft law' which is non-binding on states. As noted earlier, this situation is thus potentially problematic from two perspectives. The first of

3 For example, para. 29 of General Recommendation No. 35 asserts that states should ensure that all forms of gender-based violence against women in all spheres, including those which amount to a violation of their psychological identity, are criminalised. Article 33 of the Istanbul Convention also takes the approach that states should ensure that intentional conduct of seriously impairing a person's psychological integrity should be criminalised. Nevertheless, it was recognised that this may be problematic for particular states, therefore Article 78(3) provides that, when signing or ratifying the Istanbul Convention, a state party may declare that it reserves the right to provide for non-criminal sanctions, instead of criminal sanctions, for the behaviours referred to in Article 33. However, any state party to CEDAW may find itself subject to criticism from the CEDAW Committee for failing to criminalise violations of psychological identity, even if the state in question would not have ratified a treaty containing such a provision or would have entered a reservation in respect of it.

these relates to whether is it acceptable from the point of view of principle that there are still no legally binding standards at the international level on the issue of violence against women. The second aspect centres on the argument that the absence of legally binding provisions at the international level on violence against women makes states less responsive to the need to adopt effective measures in this area.

As regards the first aspect, it is not difficult to make the argument that it is unacceptable from the perspective of principle that there are no legally binding international provisions on violence against women. As was discussed in Chapter Two, when CEDAW was adopted in 1979 the prevalence and nature of violence against women was not understood to any great extent. However, since then there have been important developments in the understanding of this phenomenon, and it is now no longer tenable for the lack of international treaty provisions on violence against women to remain unaddressed. As Edwards comments, a treaty on violence against women 'would represent a symbolic victory to women, recognising women's equal right to human rights protection against violence within the existing system'.[4]

At present it appears that one almost has to twist CEDAW in order to attempt to make this instrument encompass the issue of gender-based violence. In an interview which former UN Special Rapporteur on violence against women, its causes and consequences, Rashida Manjoo, gave in May 2015, she commented,

> The functioning of the [CEDAW] Committee regarding violence against women is to try and fit this pervasive human rights violation under the discrimination label, and to then find ways to justify the Committee's jurisdiction by using other provisions in the CEDAW. When it receives a complaint, or when it interrogates the state parties reports, it does what I call jurisdictional gymnastics to address the issue of violence against women. It has to ask questions such as: Is violence against women discrimination? Is the violence due to stereotyping? Is it due to family relations?[5]

As Edwards remarks, 'interpretation is at best a corrective and indirect mechanism to fix the errors of the original human rights framework'[6] and should therefore be regarded as constituting only an 'interim strategy'[7] in the absence of specific treaty provisions on violence against women. Of course, it must be

4 Edwards, A., *Violence Against Women Under International Human Rights Law*, 2013, Cambridge University Press, Cambridge, 343.

5 Manjoo, R. and Nadj, D., '"Bridging the Divide": An Interview With Professor Rashida Manjoo, UN Special Rapporteur on Violence Against Women' (2015) 23 *Feminist Legal Studies* 329 at 343.

6 Edwards, op. cit., 338.

7 Edwards, op. cit., 339.

remembered that such stretching of human rights instruments is not uncommon. For example, the European Convention on Human Rights was originally designed for use by adults in resisting state power. However, this instrument is now frequently applied in instances in which the rights of one individual have been violated by another private entity.[8] Nevertheless, it appears that the adoption of a global treaty on violence against women would add substantially more force to the statements made by the CEDAW Committee and the other UN human rights bodies as regards this issue.

Do Human Rights Standards Make a Difference?

As discussed previously, it is relatively easy to see why the absence of legally binding treaty provisions at the UN level on violence against women is problematic from a perspective of principle. However, is the omission of such provisions also problematic from a practical perspective? There are essentially two inter-related issues here. These are, firstly, whether the existence of human rights standards actually makes a difference as regards the responses of states to particular issues; and secondly, if so, does it matter in terms of state responses whether the human rights standards in question are legally binding or otherwise?

As Goodman and Jinks remark, 'Fundamental to the project of international law is the assumption that legal commitments meaningfully condition the exercise of state power'.[9] The question of whether human rights treaties make a difference in practice has raised a significant amount of debate. Few detailed empirical studies have however been carried out on this question, largely due to the extensive problems involved in research of this nature. As Cassel comments, such research 'would require an enormously sophisticated methodology, coupled with a Herculean effort to gather a range of data, much of which may not exist or may not be reliable'.[10] Essentially, it is extremely difficult to establish with certainty why states change their practices as regards particular issues. As Shelton comments, 'It is very difficult to know why a state behaves as it does. . . . The causal link between state behaviour and international human rights norms is difficult to make absent direct acknowledgment

8 For example, those who drafted the European Convention on Human Rights would not have viewed a case such as *A v United Kingdom* (App. No. 25599/94, judgment of 23 September 1998) which involved a child being beaten by his stepfather, as falling within the ambit of the Convention.

9 Goodman, R. and Jinks, D., 'Measuring the Effects of Human Rights Treaties' (2003) 14 *European Journal of International Law* 171 at 171. See also Goodman, R. and Jinks, D., *Socializing States: Promoting Human Rights Through International Law*, 2013, Oxford University Press, New York.

10 Cassel, D., 'Does Human Rights Law Make a Difference?' (2001) 2 *Chicago Journal of International Law* 121 at 131.

by the state of the impact of international norms'.[11] Haas remarks, 'While the best evidence for compliance with most types of international commitments is based on changes in investment patterns and bureaucratic budgets, such evidence is often absent or extremely difficult to obtain in terms of time or money'.[12] As Charney states, 'few agree on how to calculate the rate of compliance with either "hard" or "soft" international norms'.[13]

A small number of empirical studies have nevertheless been attempted in this area, one of the most notable being that carried out by Hathaway.[14] Somewhat surprisingly, the study found 'not a single treaty for which ratification seem[ed] to be reliably associated with better human rights practices and several for which it appear[ed] to be associated with worse practices'.[15] In commenting on Hathaway's findings, Goodman and Jinks argued that the project had been flawed in its design, and that 'broad ratification of human rights treaties plays an important role in the process of building national human rights cultures'.[16] In reply, Hathaway clarified her argument, stating, 'treaties remain an indispensable tool for the promotion of human rights'[17] and 'human rights treaties can have a powerful impact on countries' human rights practices by changing discourse about rights'.[18] However, Hathaway is of the view that treaties can transform the practices not only of states which choose to ratify them, but also of the international community more generally by shaping what is understood to be acceptable practice.[19] Therefore the benefit of human rights treaties should not be measured solely on their perceived impact on the practices of states which have ratified such instruments, and thus 'the relationship between treaties and their effects may not be as simple as has been presupposed'.[20] Another empirical study on the effectiveness of

11 Shelton, D., 'Commentary and Conclusions', in Shelton, D. (ed.), *Commitment and Compliance: The Role of Non-Binding Norms in the International Legal System*, 2003, Oxford University Press, Oxford, 449 at 457.

12 Haas, P.M., 'Choosing to Comply: Theorizing from International Relations and Comparative Politics', in Shelton, D. (ed.), *Commitment and Compliance: The Role of Non-Binding Norms in the International Legal System*, 2003, Oxford University Press, Oxford, 43 at 44–45.

13 Charney, J.L., 'Compliance With International Soft Law', in Shelton, D. (ed.), *Commitment and Compliance: The Role of Non-Binding Norms in the International Legal System*, 2003, Oxford University Press, Oxford, 115 at 115.

14 Hathaway, O., 'Do Human Rights Treaties Make a Difference?' (2002) 111 *Yale Law Journal* 1935. See also, Keith, L.C., 'The United Nations International Covenant on Civil and Political Rights: Does It Make a Difference in Human Rights Behavior?' (1999) 36 *Journal of Peace Research* 95; and McCormick, J.M. and Mitchell, N.J., 'Human Rights Violations, Umbrella Concepts, and Empirical Analysis' (1997) 49 *World Politics* 510.

15 Hathaway (2002), op. cit., 1940.

16 Goodman and Jinks (2003), op. cit., 182.

17 Hathaway, O., 'Testing Conventional Wisdom' (2003) 14 *European Journal of International Law* 185 at 186.

18 Hathaway (2003), op. cit., 186.

19 Hathaway (2003), op. cit., 195.

20 Hathaway (2003), op. cit., 199.

international human rights law was carried out by Simmons,[21] who found, 'ratification of human rights treaties has had positive consequences for human rights in much of the world'.[22] According to Simmons, human rights treaties 'have touched off domestic debates, provoked demands, and raised the expectations of ordinary citizens'. They have also 'been used at crucial moments and critical junctures by litigants and judges to shape domestic law, institutions, and practices for the future'.[23]

It is certainly true that all of the existing UN human rights treaties suffer from substantial difficulties in terms of implementation and enforcement. Essentially, even if a state chooses to ratify a treaty, there is no guarantee that the state will abide by the obligations contained therein. Extensive problems with implementation and enforcement affect all of the UN human rights treaties. The implementation of international human rights law has been inconsistent, to say the least.[24] Although human rights instruments contain detailed lists of the rights which should be afforded to individuals, in many situations these rights are nevertheless still being violated. As Hafner-Burton and Tsutsui remark, 'government violation of human rights is epidemic'.[25] For human rights standards to be implemented within states, there must be a political will among governments to do so,[26] and often such a will is lacking. Copelon comments, 'the international human rights system still operates more in rhetoric than in reality'.[27] It remains the case that human rights are indeed regarded by many as rhetoric as opposed to constituting legal duties which must be observed.[28] It is extremely difficult to compel states to comply with their duties if they are reluctant to do so. As Byrnes remarks, 'The limitations of international law generally when it comes to enforcement of binding standards are well known, and international human rights law is no exception in that regard'.[29] Indeed Bayefsky comments that the large numbers of ratifications of the UN human rights treaties 'reflect the widely-held

21 Simmons, B.A., *Mobilizing for Human Rights: International Law in Domestic Politics*, 2009, Cambridge University Press, New York.

22 Simmons, op. cit., 380.

23 Simmons, op. cit., 351.

24 Wallace, R., *International Human Rights*, 2001, Sweet & Maxwell, London, 589.

25 Hafner-Burton, E.M. and Tsutsui, K., 'Human Rights in a Globalizing World: The Paradox of Empty Promises' (2005) 110 *American Journal of Sociology* 1373 at 1374.

26 Wallace, op. cit., 590.

27 Copelon, R., 'International Human Rights Dimensions of Intimate Violence: Another Strand in the Dialectic of Feminist Lawmaking' (2003) 11 *American University Journal of Gender, Social Policy and the Law* 865 at 875.

28 Robinson, M., 'Making Human Rights Matter: Eleanor Roosevelt's Time Has Come' (2003) 16 *Harvard Human Rights Journal* 1 at 1.

29 Byrnes, A., 'Enforcement Through International Law and Procedures', in Cook, R.J. (ed.), *Human Rights of Women – National and International Perspectives*, 1994, University of Pennsylvania Press, Philadelphia, 189 at 191–192.

view by states parties that there are not serious consequences associated with ratification'.[30]

It appears that this failure may be due at least partly to the 'lack of an international policing force that demands compliance with international edicts'.[31] The UN has no real method of forcing states to alter their policies. It must instead attempt to persuade nations to comply with their international duties.[32] Risse and Sikkink remark, 'Countries most sensitive to pressure are not those that are economically weakest, but those that care about their international image'.[33] However, if a government is powerful on an international scale, it may be impervious to international human rights law.[34] Merry comments,

> Countries are concerned about their reputations in the international community, but they clearly differ in their vulnerability to international pressure depending on their size, wealth, form of government, and dependence on the international community for trade, aid, and other symbolic and material forms of exchange.[35]

The effectiveness of human rights treaties therefore depends greatly on the level of commitment held by states to give effect to their duties. As Crawford remarks, 'There are no doubt inherent problems with a system for human rights protection based essentially on self-criticism and good faith'.[36] Egan comments that the UN treaty bodies, national human rights institutions and non-governmental organisations 'face a task of Sisyphean proportions in coaxing States to implement the treaty body recommendations'.[37]

Ulrich remarks that the difficulties relating to implementation and enforcement are magnified as regards treaties which address women's rights.[38] For example, in relation to CEDAW, Schopp-Schilling asserts, 'many States Parties

30 Bayefsky, A.F., *The UN Human Rights Treaty System: Universality at the Crossroads*, 2001, Transnational Publishers, Ardsley, 7.

31 Ulrich, J., 'Confronting Gender-Based Violence With International Instruments: Is a Solution to the Pandemic Within Reach?' (2000) 7 *Indiana Journal of Global Legal Studies* 629 at 637.

32 Ulrich, op. cit., 638–639.

33 Risse, T. and Sikkink, K., 'The socialization of international human rights norms into domestic practices: introduction', in Risse, T., Ropp, S.C. and Sikkink, K. (eds.), *The Power of Human Rights – International Norms and Domestic Change*, 1999, Cambridge University Press, Cambridge, 1 at 37–38.

34 Cassel, op. cit., 135.

35 Merry, S.E., 'Constructing a Global Law – Violence Against Women and the Human Rights System' (2003) 28 *Law and Social Inquiry* 941 at 959.

36 Crawford, J., 'The UN Human Rights Treaty System: A System in Crisis?', in Alston, P. and Crawford, J. (eds.), *The Future of UN Human Rights Treaty Monitoring*, 2000, Cambridge University Press, Cambridge, 1 at 7.

37 Egan, S., *The UN Human Rights Treaty System: Law and Procedure*, 2011, Bloomsbury Professional, Dublin, 477.

38 Ulrich, op. cit.638.

have often not addressed issues of legal reform or programmes to improve the material situation of women to enable and empower them to claim, exercise and enjoy their human rights, even if they ratified the CEDAW 15 or 20 years ago'.[39] Merry comments, 'CEDAW is law without sanctions'.[40] Ritz asserts, 'CEDAW . . . has proven ineffective in ending gender discrimination'.[41] Afsharipour remarks, 'due to a lack of effective enforcement mechanisms, the Convention's success in improving the lives of women has been limited'.[42] Essentially, it is clear that, despite the fact that CEDAW has been ratified by a very large number of states,[43] gender inequality still persists.

If legally binding treaty provisions on violence against women were to be adopted within the UN framework, it is highly probable that the primary monitoring mechanism would be a reporting mechanism similar to those used by the other UN human rights treaties, such as CEDAW. However, the difficulties associated with such mechanisms are substantial and pertain to the reporting procedures of all of the existing UN treaties. The implementation problems suffered by the UN human rights treaties have been exacerbated by difficulties surrounding the reporting procedures, which constitute the primary monitoring mechanisms of these instruments.[44] Egan comments,

> Many States appear to ignore totally the guidelines which the treaty bodies have produced to assist them in preparing their reports. The quality of the reports can range from being inadequate to blatantly derisory. Formal presentation of the report in the public sessions can often serve to reinforce the impression that the process is not taken seriously by many governments, or is at best regarded as an obligatory, but essentially shallow, diplomatic exercise.[45]

Fortin remarks,

> the reporting mechanism relies on governments to subject their implementation programme to an objective and critical analysis before compiling

39 Schopp-Schilling, H.B., 'Treaty Body Reform: The Case of the Committee on the Elimination of Discrimination Against Women' (2007) 7 *Human Rights Law Review* 201 at 204.

40 Merry, op. cit., 943.

41 Ritz, K.L., 'Soft Enforcement: Inadequacies of Optional Protocol as a Remedy for the Convention on the Elimination of All Forms of Discrimination Against Women' (2001) 25 *Suffolk Transnational Law Review* 191 at 193.

42 Afsharipour A., 'Empowering Ourselves: The Role of Women's NGOs in the Enforcement of the Women's Convention' (1999) 99 *Columbia Law Review* 129 at 129.

43 At the time of writing, 189 states have ratified CEDAW.

44 For discussion generally of the reporting procedures of the UN human rights treaties, see Kalin, W., 'Examination of state reports', in Keller, H. and Ulfstein, G. (eds.), *UN Human Rights Treaty Bodies – Law and Legitimacy*, 2012, Cambridge University Press, Cambridge, 16.

45 Egan, op. cit., 172–173.

> their reports. The absence of any supervision or coercion over this can lead to reports painting an over-optimistic and complacent picture of governmental achievements.[46]

Smith comments, 'The reports system is often regarded as weak because it is dependent upon the will of States to comply. . . . Self-appraisal may be entering mainstream management practice in the developed world but it has yet to reach mainstream international law'.[47] In relation to CEDAW, Merry sets out seven methods by which states may escape proper scrutiny by the CEDAW Committee.[48] Firstly, the state may fail to write a report or do so only after a long delay. Secondly, the state may write only a superficial report. Thirdly, the state may send only low-level government representatives to present the report. Fourthly, the state may avoid answering questions directly. Fifthly, the state may promise to make changes but fail to act on such promises. Sixthly, the state may enter extensive reservations, and lastly the state may refuse to present its report even after submission. Often states submit their reports only after long delays, and there is also a backlog in relation to the consideration of reports by the CEDAW Committee, which further adds to the delays. As Rehman comments,

> The present reporting procedure as provided in the [CEDAW] Convention, in common with other reporting procedures, has proved less than satisfactory. Reports are often delayed, out-dated and inadequate, with most State parties placing emphasis upon the legislative mechanisms relating to gender equality.[49]

Essentially, 'The realisation of the purposes and principles set forth in the Convention through a system of periodic reporting has not been satisfactory'.[50] As Lacey states, 'The critical dialogue potentially set up by CEDAW is, inevitably, distorted at every turn by the realities of political, cultural, and economic power'.[51]

46 Fortin, J., *Children's Rights and the Developing Law*, 2003, Butterworths, London, 46. Although this comment was made in the context of a discussion of the UN Convention on the Rights of the Child, the statement applies equally to the reporting mechanisms under the other UN human rights treaties.

47 Smith, R.K.M., *Textbook on International Human Rights*, 6th ed., 2014, Oxford University Press, Oxford, 165.

48 Merry, op. cit., 958.

49 Rehman, J., *International Human Rights Law*, 2nd ed., 2010, Pearson Education Limited, Harlow, 538–539.

50 Rehman, op. cit., 554.

51 Lacey, N., 'Feminist Legal Theory and the Rights of Women', in Knop, K. (ed.), *Gender and Human Rights*, 2004, Oxford University Press, Oxford, 13 at 54.

In addition, the problems are not of course confined only to the responses of states to their reporting obligations. The treaty monitoring bodies themselves work under great pressures in terms of attempting to consider the reports submitted in the limited time which is available. Even though states frequently submit their reports late, when the reports are submitted they may not be considered by the treaty monitoring bodies for some time, due to backlogs of reports in the system. Indeed if all states submitted all of their reports in time, it is probable that the reporting mechanisms would simply collapse due to the inability of the treaty monitoring bodies to cope with the vast numbers of reports to be considered.

Due to these problems, none of the international treaties work at the optimal level of effectiveness. Despite the existence of these instruments, breaches of human rights law still frequently occur. However, acceptance of this fact is very different to saying that human rights law is ineffective or has only minimal utility. Human rights law has undoubtedly accomplished a great deal within what is a relatively short space of time. As Robinson comments,

> Starting with the Universal Declaration and carried forward in the body of international law that has been painstakingly developed over half a century, the world has expressed through human rights its shared commitment to the values of dignity, equality, and human security for all people.[52]

Cassel remarks, 'International articulation of rights norms has reshaped domestic dialogues in law, politics, academia, public consciousness, civil society, and the press'.[53] Essentially, international human rights law has been utilised to establish standards which go beyond national barriers and has exposed to external scrutiny abuses which would otherwise have remained exclusively the concern of the states wherein they were carried out.

It can thus be stated that 'human rights are now firmly on the agenda of the international community'.[54] Human rights law has delineated the principles by which governments should act, and the governments of most states now generally accept these principles. As Risse and Ropp comment, 'transnational human rights pressures and policies . . . have made a very significant difference in bringing about improvements in human rights practices in diverse countries around the world'.[55] Although difficult to prove empirically, '[t]he utility of international human rights law is merely one of many international policy

52 Robinson, op. cit., 1.

53 Cassel, op. cit., 122.

54 Robinson, op. cit., 4.

55 Risse, T. and Ropp, S.C., 'International Human Rights Norms and Domestic Change: Conclusions', in Risse, T., Ropp, S.C. and Sikkink, K. (eds.), *The Power of Human Rights – International Norms and Domestic Change*, 1999, Cambridge University Press, Cambridge, 234 at 275.

questions that must rely mainly on judgment informed by experience'.[56] It seems therefore fair to conclude that the existence of human rights standards do make a significant difference as regards how states respond to particular issues.

Does It Matter Whether Human Rights Standards Are Legally Binding or 'Soft Law'?

Does it matter however from a practical perspective whether the standards in question are legally binding or otherwise? Essentially, would the responses of states to the issue of violence against women be improved if the international human rights standards in this area were legally binding, as opposed to being 'soft law'? The utility of 'soft law', relative to legally binding standards, is also an issue which has attracted some debate. It seems that although soft law can certainly be beneficial,

> it is also clear that, from earliest times, states and other social actors have found it useful to draw a relatively sharp distinction between norms and normative arrangements that are meant to be binding, backed up by the organized community's authority, and those that are not.[57]

O'Connell states, 'despite all of its utility, soft law is not confused with hard law; the aim of most in global governance is to get enforceable hard law obligations'.[58] Cassel comments, 'Formally obligatory international norms can legitimize and fortify the organizing and consciousness-raising efforts of non-governmental organizations'.[59] As Bilder remarks, 'there remains a widely-held and long understood assumption in all societies that there *is* a meaningful difference between norms that are intended to be legally binding and those that are not, and that people may rely on this difference' (emphasis original).[60] Shelton comments, 'In the long run . . . non-binding norms in human rights are generally not as effective as binding commitments and the

56 Cassel, op. cit., 124.

57 Bilder, R.B., 'Beyond Compliance: Helping Nations Cooperate', in Shelton, D. (ed.), *Commitment and Compliance: The Role of Non-Binding Norms in the International Legal System*, 2003, Oxford University Press, Oxford, 65 at 71.

58 O'Connell, M.E., 'The Role of Soft Law in a Global Order', in Shelton, D. (ed.), *Commitment and Compliance: The Role of Non-Binding Norms in the International Legal System*, 2003, Oxford University Press, Oxford, 100 at 111.

59 Cassel, op. cit., 122.

60 Bilder, op. cit., 71–72.

enforcement possibilities that come with them for victims and their representatives'.[61] Simmons states,

> Treaties are the clearest statements available about the content of globally sanctioned decent rights practices. . . . Treaties serve notice that governments are *accountable* – domestically and externally – for refraining from the abuses proscribed by their own mutual agreements. Treaties signal a seriousness of intent that is difficult to replicate in other ways (emphasis original).[62]

In 2007, research was carried out which addressed the issue of how states have responded to the comments of the CEDAW Committee on the issue of domestic abuse in which 11 western European states were examined.[63] It was found that the majority of the states surveyed, including states such as Denmark, Germany, Ireland, Italy, Norway and Spain, were complying with only some of the recommendations of the Committee as regards this issue. Certain states, such as Luxembourg, the Netherlands and Sweden, did seem to be complying with most of the Committee's recommendations. However, as was noted in the study, it is difficult to ascertain whether the measures adopted by such states were as a result of the comments made by the CEDAW Committee or whether they were due to other factors, such as pressure being exerted by non-governmental organisations or by academic commentators.

Another study which was carried out in 2011 examined the implementation in the UK of the recommendations made by the international human rights bodies on domestic abuse.[64] Again it was found that these statements suffer from great difficulties as regards their effectiveness. The recommendations had not been uniformly implemented in the UK, and it appeared that the primary reason for this was a lack of will on the part of the state, combined with a lack of enforcement mechanisms. Notably, the most problematic area in relation to the government's response to domestic abuse was found to be the provision of social support measures to victims, which is the category of recommendations which necessitates the greatest amount of money to be spent. The study found that even in areas in which the UK did appear to be

61 Shelton, op. cit., 463. See also Klabbers, J., 'The Redundancy of Soft Law' (1996) 65 *Nordic Journal of International Law* 167; Ingelse, C., 'Soft Law' (1993) 20 *Polish Yearbook of International Law* 75; and Weil, P., 'Towards Relative Normativity in International Law?' (1983) 77 *American Journal of International Law* 413. Further, for discussion of the use of indicators, see Merry, S.E. (ed.), *The Quiet Power of Indicators: Measuring Governance, Corruption, and Rule of Law*, 2015, Cambridge University Press, Cambridge.

62 Simmons, op. cit., 4–5.

63 McQuigg, R., 'The Responses of States to the Comments of the CEDAW Committee on Domestic Violence' (2007) 11 *International Journal of Human Rights* 461.

64 McQuigg, R., *International Human Rights Law and Domestic Violence*, 2011, Routledge, Abingdon, 99–124.

fulfilling the recommendations of the international human rights bodies, at least to some extent, such as in relation to improving the criminal justice system, it seemed that changes in government policy were more likely to have been due to other factors, such as pressure from academic commentators and non-governmental organisations.

The former UN Special Rapporteur on violence against women, its causes and consequences, Rashida Manjoo, has made a compelling case for the need for legally binding standards on violence against women, based upon her own experiences as Special Rapporteur. In a report of May 2014 to the UN Human Rights Council, she stated, 'although soft laws may be influential in developing norms, their non-binding nature effectively means that states cannot be held responsible for violations'. She proceeded to note, 'none of the soft law developments on violence against women has moved into the realm of customary international law as yet'.[65]

Since then Manjoo has made various statements in which she strongly expresses her view that the adoption of a legally binding treaty at the international level is an absolute necessity in order for states to be held accountable as regards their responses to violence against women. For example, in a report presented to the UN General Assembly in September 2014, she stated,

> Although many States have acknowledged violence against women as a widespread and systematic human rights violation and are working on eradicating it, to differing degrees at the national level, the normative gap within international human rights law as regards violence against women is a barrier to holding States accountable for the failure to respect, protect and fulfil the human rights of women.[66]

Likewise, in an interview which Manjoo gave in May 2015, she stated, 'having a specific treaty on violence against women would provide for a dedicated accountability mechanism i.e. a mechanism that would hold states accountable more stringently to standards that are clearly articulated including being specific about State obligations'.[67]

65 Report of the Special Rapporteur on Violence Against Women, its causes and consequences, U.N. Doc. A/HRC/26/38, 28 May 2014, at para. 68.

66 Report of the Special Rapporteur on Violence Against Women, its causes and consequences to the UN General Assembly, U.N. Doc. A/69/368, 1 September 2014, at para. 68.

67 Manjoo and Nadj, op. cit., 343.

In a similar vein, the primary focus of Manjoo's final report as Special Rapporteur was on the necessity of adopting a UN treaty on violence against women. In this report she asserted,

> The normative gap under international human rights law raises crucial questions about the State responsibility to act with due diligence and the responsibility of the State as the ultimate duty bearer to protect women and girls from violence, its causes and consequences. . . . Given the systemic, widespread and pervasive nature of this human rights violation, which is experienced largely by women because they are women, a different set of normative and practical measures to respond to, prevent and ultimately eliminate such violence is crucial.[68]

It seems that such strong statements on the need to adopt legally binding standards at the UN level on violence against women cannot be lightly disregarded.

It is also notable that in 2011 the Council of Europe adopted a Convention on Preventing and Combating Violence Against Women and Domestic Violence (the Istanbul Convention), and that in 2025 the African Union (AU) adopted the Convention on Ending Violence Against Women and Girls, despite the fact that all of the member states of both the Council of Europe and the AU were already parties to CEDAW and were therefore subject to the 'soft law' standards developed by the CEDAW Committee and the other UN bodies in this area. Few of the measures found among the provisions of the Istanbul Convention or the AU Convention are new – most had been previously articulated by the CEDAW Committee and other UN bodies. Nevertheless, the Council of Europe and the AU saw fit to put these standards in the format of treaties, thereby making them legally binding. If the Council of Europe or the AU had been of the view that it was of no consequence whether these standards were merely 'soft law' or were of a legally binding nature, there would have been little or no point in adopting these Conventions. The very existence of these instruments is evidence of support for the argument that human rights standards need to be legally binding in order for them to attain a sufficient degree of efficacy.[69]

The Merits of an International Approach

The existence of the Istanbul Convention and the AU Convention does however raise another question regarding the merits of treaty provisions at the UN

68 Report of the Special Rapporteur on Violence Against Women, its causes and consequences, Rashida Manjoo, UN. Doc. A/HRC/29/27, 10 June 2015, at para. 63.

69 For further discussion of the Istanbul Convention, see McQuigg, R., *The Istanbul Convention, Domestic Violence and Human Rights*, 2017, Routledge, Abingdon.

level on violence against women. Is this issue best dealt with at the global level or is a regional approach more advantageous? Notably, these Conventions are not the only regional treaties on violence against women. Within the Inter-American system of human rights protection, the Inter-American Convention on the Prevention, Punishment and Eradication of Violence Against Women (also known as the Convention of Belém do Pará), was adopted as far back as 1994. Is this issue therefore best addressed by regional instruments such as these?

The existence of regional standards on violence against women is certainly meritorious, and it is possible that regional instruments may have advantages over international treaties as regards enforcement. As Smith remarks, 'There may be a greater political will to conform to regional texts as they are sometimes seen as being of more immediate concern than the international initiatives'.[70] Nevertheless, the fact that there are a number of legally binding provisions on violence against women within the context of regional systems of human rights protection by no means eliminates the need for such provisions at the UN level. Firstly, there are huge swathes of the globe which do not fall within any of the regional systems of human rights protection which encompass treaty provisions on this issue. Also, the regional provisions on violence against women which are currently in existence vary dramatically in terms of scope. For example, the Istanbul Convention places extremely extensive and detailed duties on states parties. By contrast, the AU Convention and the Convention of Belém do Pará place considerably less detailed obligations on states parties. There is thus a need for a uniform set of obligations to be adopted.

Can it nonetheless be argued that issues relating to violence against women vary between regions and therefore that the development of regional approaches would be more suitable than the adoption of a global treaty on violence against women? It is true that the specific issues relating to violence against women can vary to some extent between regions and indeed between states, for example, as regards the prevalence of particular types of violence. As Merry comments, 'Gender violence occurs throughout the world, but it takes quite different forms in different social contexts'.[71] However, gender-based violence, no matter what form it takes, tends to be rooted in the same concepts – those of power and control. Also, to argue that violence against women is an issue which is more appropriately addressed at a regional level runs a substantial risk of straying into the problematic realms of cultural relativism. 'Arguments about preserving culture become the basis

70 Smith, op. cit., 88.

71 Merry, S.E., *Gender Violence – A Cultural Perspective*, 2009, Wiley-Blackwell, Chichester, 3.

for defending male control over women.'[72] Human rights are universal, and a universal set of legally binding standards on violence against women are therefore needed. This set of standards could of course be supplemented if necessary by further regional instruments if there are issues in certain areas which are particularly problematic.

Would States Ratify a Legally Binding UN Instrument on Violence Against Women?

Perhaps one of the most fundamental questions relating to whether a legally binding UN instrument on violence against women should be adopted is the very practical issue of would a significant number of states actually choose to ratify such an instrument?[73] It is of course impossible to reach a definitive answer to this question, and any analysis of the likelihood of states ratifying such a treaty can only be speculative in nature. Rashida Manjoo has expressed the view that one of the primary reasons that such an instrument has not yet been adopted is a lack of political will.[74] However, it could perhaps be questioned whether this is in fact the case. It is notable that the large majority of states within the Council of Europe have ratified the Istanbul Convention.[75] In addition, the Convention of Belém do Pará is the most widely ratified convention within the Inter-American system.[76] The favourable responses by states to these regional Conventions on violence against women seems to indicate that a large number of states may in fact be willing to ratify a binding instrument at the UN level on violence against women.

The degree of willingness among states to ratify such an instrument would clearly depend to a great extent on the nature of the obligations to be found therein. The more extensive and onerous these obligations are, the less likely it is that states will ratify. However, it would of course be necessary to ensure that the provisions of such an instrument were not too weak as to be ineffective. In drafting such provisions, a very careful balance would therefore need to be struck in this regard.

Another important issue is that of resources. Addressing violence against women in as effective a manner as possible requires expenditure of state resources. For example, a number of the measures found in the Istanbul

72 Merry, S.E., *Human Rights and Gender Violence*, 2006, University of Chicago Press, Chicago, 25.

73 For discussion of why states ratify human rights treaties, see for example, Simmons, op. cit., 57–111.

74 Manjoo and Nadj, op. cit. 343.

75 At the time of writing, 38 states have ratified the Istanbul Convention, and another six states have signed, but not yet ratified, the Convention. Azerbaijan is the only member state of the Council of Europe which has neither ratified nor signed this instrument.

76 There are currently 32 states parties to the Convention of Belém do Pará.

Convention, such as those relating to the support services which should be made available to victims,[77] require states to expend substantial levels of monetary resources. However, many of the wealthiest states globally can be found in Europe. Including similar obligations in a global instrument on violence against women may result in low rates of ratification. The governments of many states may feel that they simply do not have sufficient resources to comply with such duties, particularly in the current economic climate. It is notable that the obligations found in the AU Convention are significantly less detailed than those which are placed on states parties to the Istanbul Convention. Indeed the Istanbul Convention consists of 81 articles, as opposed to the 20 articles which comprise the AU Convention. For example, considerably more detail is provided in the Istanbul Convention on the duties of states parties in relation to aspects such awareness-raising; education; training of professionals; preventive intervention and treatment programmes; the provision of shelters and telephone helplines; protection and support for child witnesses; civil lawsuits and remedies; psychological violence; stalking; and forced marriage. Nevertheless, the drafters of the AU Convention chose to articulate the obligations of states parties in a substantially more general manner. It is probable that this approach may have been due, at least in part, to issues surrounding resources. Detailed duties such as those contained in the Istanbul Convention require considerable amounts of resources to implement, and many of the world's poorest countries are to be found in Africa. Although it is of course the case that implementing the obligations found in the AU Convention would also require expenditure on the part of states, it is likely that this would be to a significantly lesser extent. Essentially, the fact that the duties placed upon states parties by the AU Convention are so much less detailed than those contained in the Istanbul Convention serves to indicate that it is highly improbable that an instrument of a similar level of detail to that of the Istanbul Convention would be adopted at the global level.

It was an understanding of the low levels of resources of many states globally which led to the concept of 'progressive realisation' being included in the International Covenant on Economic, Social and Cultural Rights (ICESCR), under which ratification does not mean that states must immediately comply with all of the provisions of this instrument. Instead, states are under a duty to realise their obligations progressively, in accordance with available monetary resources.[78] Nevertheless, as regards an issue such as violence against women, would an instrument which did not, for example, place duties on states to provide sufficient social support measures for victims actually be meaningful? For example, in relation to domestic abuse, it is often measures of social

77 See Istanbul Convention, Chapter IV – Protection and Support.

78 See Article 2(1) of the ICESCR.

support which are of most importance to victims.[79] Likewise, if such obligations were encompassed in a global instrument and the concept of progressive realisation were also included, would this dilute these duties to such an extent as to make them ineffective? These are difficult questions to which there are no straightforward answers.

Another issue relating to the likelihood of states ratifying a binding UN instrument on violence against women lies in the question of what approach would be taken towards reservations in any such instrument. The approach which should be adopted towards reservations by any new instrument is a difficult issue. Essentially, a balance must be struck between, on the one hand, the desire to ensure that as many states as possible ratify the instrument in question and thus permitting some leeway in order to encourage them to do so, and on the other hand, ensuring that states are not allowed to enter reservations which are so extensive that they impact on the very heart of the instrument itself. It is not easy to strike this balance in the correct manner. For example, although CEDAW is one of the most widely ratified of the UN treaties, it is also the treaty to which the most reservations, and indeed the most extensive reservations, have been entered by states parties. It is arguable that the approach which has been adopted towards reservations under CEDAW has been of too lenient a nature. Article 28 of CEDAW permits ratification subject to reservations, provided the reservations are not incompatible with the object and purpose of CEDAW.[80] It appears though that a broad approach is adopted towards compatibility. Rehman remarks, 'Out of all the human rights treaties, the Women's Convention has attracted the highest number of reservations, some of them so sweeping and overriding in nature that the issue of good faith and principle of integrity of the instrument inevitably comes into question'.[81] Likewise, Cook comments, 'the legal issue of the propriety of reservations to this Convention goes to the heart of both values of universality and integrity'.[82] Similarly, Rehman is of the view that 'the significant number of reservations do pose a serious challenge'.[83] Isa states that the high number of reservations to CEDAW constitutes 'A serious problem that has had a profound impact on the effectiveness of CEDAW'.[84] Likewise, Smith

79 Schneider, E.M., *Battered Women & Feminist Lawmaking*, 2000, Yale University Press, New Haven, 196–197.

80 Article 28(2) states, 'A reservation incompatible with the object and purpose of the present Convention shall not be permitted'.

81 Rehman, op. cit., 554.

82 Cook, R.J., 'Reservations to the Convention on the Elimination of All Forms of Discrimination Against Women' (1989–1990) 30 *Virginia Journal of International Law* 643 at 644.

83 Rehman, op. cit., 536.

84 Isa, F.G., 'The Optional Protocol for the Convention on the Elimination of All Forms of Discrimination Against Women: Strengthening the Protection of Women's Human Rights' (2003) 20 *Arizona Journal of International and Comparative Law* 291 at 302.

remarks that CEDAW is 'beset by problems due to the extraordinarily high number of reservations thereto'.[85] Although these reservations are widely regarded as being immensely problematic, the approach which was adopted in this regard was that it was preferable to allow states to ratify CEDAW with extensive reservations rather than such states not ratifying the Convention at all. Nevertheless, if a substantial number of states were only persuaded to ratify CEDAW because they were permitted to enter extensive reservations, it may be unlikely that such states would ratify an instrument on violence against women without similarly being allowed to enter substantive reservations. However, would the permitting of such reservations again dilute such an instrument so as to make it of little practical value? Again, this is a key question which would necessitate detailed consideration prior to the adoption of any global instrument on violence against women.

Conclusion

When CEDAW was drafted in 1979, violence against women was simply not an issue on the agenda for international human rights law. Awareness and understanding of the extent of this issue, and of its complex and multi-faceted nature, has nonetheless grown enormously in recent years. If an instrument focusing on the rights of women were to be adopted in the present day, it would simply be inconceivable for an issue such as violence against women to be omitted. Although violence against women is now clearly on the agenda of UN bodies such as the CEDAW Committee, it is unjustifiable from the perspective of principle that there are still no legally binding provisions at the international level on this issue. This situation is also problematic from a practical perspective, in that it creates difficulties in terms of holding states accountable as regards their responses to violence against women.

Certainly the development of a binding UN instrument on this issue would be by no means an easy process. On the contrary, there are many issues which would require painstaking examination. As discussed previously in this chapter, all of the UN human rights treaties suffer from substantial problems as regards their implementation and enforcement. This raises the question therefore of how difficulties of this nature could be avoided in respect of a binding UN instrument on violence against women. It is almost certain that the answer is that they could not. The question which would thus necessitate extensive consideration prior to the adoption of any global instrument on violence against women is how such problems could be minimised as far as possible. Other issues which would require substantial examination include how best to strike a balance between, on the one hand, making state obligations under

85 Smith, op. cit., 164.

such an instrument as effective and detailed as possible, and on the other, not making such duties so onerous that states would be discouraged from ratification. Nevertheless, although there would certainly be many difficult issues to be addressed in the process, it is now time for the development and adoption of binding provisions at the UN level on violence against women.

The book will therefore proceed to examine the form which should be taken by such provisions. One possibility would be the adoption of an Optional Protocol to CEDAW on violence against women, as will be analysed in Chapter Four. Chapter Five will then examine another form which legally binding provisions at the UN level on violence against women could take, namely a stand-alone treaty on violence against women.

4 An Optional Protocol to CEDAW on Violence Against Women

The book now proceeds to examine the form which should be taken by legally binding standards at the UN level on violence against women. The first possibility would be the adoption of an Optional Protocol to CEDAW on this issue, as will now be analysed in Chapter Four. In December 2023, the current UN Special Rapporteur on violence against women, its causes and consequences, Reem Alsalem, along with two previous holders of this mandate, Dubravka Šimonović[1] and Rashida Manjoo,[2] issued a joint call for states to consider strongly the adoption of such an Optional Protocol. As will be discussed in this chapter, the adoption of an Optional Protocol to CEDAW on violence against women to be monitored by the CEDAW Committee would be likely to be substantially less costly than the adoption of a stand-alone treaty and the establishment of a separate monitoring body. Also, this approach would carry less of a reporting burden for states. In addition, the possible content of a potential Optional Protocol will be examined.

Call by the Current and Former UN Special Rapporteurs on Violence Against Women for Consideration of the Adoption of an Optional Protocol to CEDAW on Violence Against Women

In December 2023, the current UN Special Rapporteur on violence against women, Reem Alsalem, along with two previous holders of this mandate, Dubravka Šimonović and Rashida Manjoo, issued a joint call for states to consider strongly the adoption of an Optional Protocol to CEDAW on violence

1 Dubravka Šimonović held the mandate of UN Special Rapporteur on violence against women, its causes and consequences from 2015 until 2021.

2 Rashida Manjoo held the mandate of UN Special Rapporteur on violence against women, its causes and consequences from 2009 until 2015.

DOI: 10.4324/9781003603689-4

against women.[3] In this statement the current and former Special Rapporteurs expressed their view that 'Now is the time for an optional protocol to CEDAW on violence against women and girls'. In support of this assertion, they cited the statistic that an estimated 736 million women globally have been subjected to domestic abuse or other sexual violence at least once. This figure equates to 30 per cent of women aged 15 and older, and in most cases, violence against women is perpetrated by current or former husbands or partners. The statement also asserted that women and girls continue to be subjected to femicide, or gender-related killings, around the globe.

The statement proceeded to comment that CEDAW and the CEDAW Committee have 'played an important role in ensuring that the term discrimination against women implicitly covers violence against women' through the use of General Recommendations Nos. 19[4] and 35.[5] However,

> while the General Recommendations provide authoritative interpretations of CEDAW and guidance for States parties on the implementation of their obligations under the Convention, the much-needed improvements in law and in practice to address violence against women at the national level, have yet to take effect'.

The current and former Special Rapporteurs also acknowledged the 'importance and the impact' of regional treaties on violence against women, and stated that such instruments 'have gone a long way in defining the different forms of violence that all women and girls may experience' as well as in seeking accountability and redress for survivors of such violence. Indeed the current and former Special Rapporteurs were of the view that 'regional human rights instruments and mechanisms that are tailored to the needs and realities of the region continue to be vital for advancing gender equality, non-discrimination and accountability', and the statement called upon states to ratify such treaties where applicable and to apply their provisions in a robust manner.

Nevertheless, the current and former Special Rapporteurs proceeded to state,

> history has shown that the lack of a universally accepted legal framework that explicitly defines and spells out the various forms of violence against

3 Statement by current and former Special Rapporteurs on violence against women, its causes and consequences, 'Now Is the Time for an Optional Protocol to CEDAW on Violence Against Women and Girls', 7 December 2023, available at https://www.ohchr.org/sites/default/files/documents/issues/women/sr/statements/stm-op-vaw-sr-vaw-7-12-23.pdf.

4 Committee on the Elimination of Discrimination Against Women, U.N. Doc. A/47/38 (1992).

5 Committee on the Elimination of Discrimination Against Women, CEDAW/C/GC/35 (2017).

> women, criminalizes it, sets out prevention and protection measures and entitles victims to reparations, continues to be a principal stumbling block that must be overcome.

Indeed, the realities of discrimination and violence against women 'have been aggravated by the onset of additional global challenges, including among others, the COVID-19 crisis, the proliferation of conflict, and climate change'. In addition, the statement commented, 'women are being subjected to new and emerging forms of violence' including in the online sphere, which not only affect 'their lives, safety, dignity, and freedom, but their equal and full participation in society as a whole'.

For these reasons, the current and former Special Rapporteurs were of the view that 'a global treaty dedicated to ending gender-based violence against women would constitute a timely and effective way of advancing gender equality and non-discrimination, ending violence and achieving greater accountability and justice for crimes committed against women and girls'. The statement proceeded to assert,

> To ensure that minimum global standards on women's rights are not further compromised, but are upheld and strengthened, it would be essential for this global treaty to be attached to CEDAW as an optional protocol, whereby it would provide an explicit legally binding roadmap on the measures needed to combat and prevent violence against women, and trigger much needed changes at the national level to secure every woman's right to live a life free from violence.

The current and former Special Rapporteurs therefore invited UN member states, the CEDAW Committee, other regional and international human rights mechanisms addressing discrimination and violence against women and girls, and other relevant actors such as defenders of women's human rights and women-led organisations to embark on a process of reflection on the content and objective of such an instrument.

Interesting comparisons can be drawn between this statement and comments made previously by the two former Special Rapporteurs concerning their views on the necessity or otherwise for the adoption of legally binding standards at the UN level on violence against women. As was discussed in Chapter Three, in a number of statements made during her tenure as Special Rapporteur, Rashida Manjoo strongly expressed her firm belief that legally binding standards at the global level on violence against women were essential to addressing this issue sufficiently. Indeed, Manjoo made a compelling case for the need for such standards, based upon her own experiences as Special Rapporteur. For example, in a report of May 2014 to the UN Human Rights Council, she stated, 'although soft laws may be influential in developing norms, their non-binding nature effectively means that states cannot be held responsible for violations'. She proceeded to note, 'none of the soft law developments on violence against women has moved into the realm of customary international law as yet'.[6] She also commented,

> Despite the existence of interpretative guidelines and monitoring by human rights treaty bodies . . . the limitations of large and varied mandates, coupled with time constraints when examining State party reports, result in insufficient interrogation concerning the information relating to violence against women, its causes and consequences, and insufficient assessment of responses.[7]

Likewise, in a report presented to the UN General Assembly in September 2014, Manjoo stated,

> Although many States have acknowledged violence against women as a widespread and systematic human rights violation and are working on eradicating it, to differing degrees at the national level, the normative gap within international human rights law as regards violence against women is a barrier to holding States accountable for the failure to respect, protect and fulfil the human rights of women.[8]

Similarly, in an interview which Manjoo gave in May 2015, she stated, 'having a specific treaty on violence against women would provide for a dedicated accountability mechanism i.e. a mechanism that would hold states accountable more stringently to standards that are clearly articulated including being specific about State obligations'.[9] In the same interview, Manjoo commented,

> The functioning of the [CEDAW] Committee regarding violence against women is to try and fit this pervasive human rights violation under the discrimination label, and to then find ways to justify the Committee's jurisdiction by using other provisions in the CEDAW. When it receives a complaint, or when it interrogates the state parties reports, it does what I call jurisdictional gymnastics to address the issue of violence against women.

6 Report of the Special Rapporteur on Violence Against Women, its causes and consequences, U.N. Doc. A/HRC/26/38, 28 May 2014, at para. 68.

7 Report of the Special Rapporteur on violence against women, its causes and consequences, Rashida Manjoo, U.N. Doc. A/HRC/26/38, 28 May 2014, at para. 76.

8 Report of the Special Rapporteur on Violence Against Women, its causes and consequences to the UN General Assembly, U.N. Doc. A/69/368, 1 September 2014, at para. 68.

9 Manjoo, R. and Nadj, D., '"Bridging the Divide": An Interview With Professor Rashida Manjoo, UN Special Rapporteur on Violence Against Women' (2015) 23 *Feminist Legal Studies* 329 at 343.

> It has to ask questions such as: Is violence against women discrimination? Is the violence due to stereotyping? Is it due to family relations?[10]

Manjoo was of the view that one of the primary reasons that a UN treaty on violence against women had not yet been adopted was a lack of political will.[11]

In a similar vein, the primary focus of Manjoo's final report as Special Rapporteur was on the necessity for the adoption of legally binding standards at the UN level on violence against women. In this report she asserted,

> The normative gap under international human rights law raises crucial questions about the State responsibility to act with due diligence and the responsibility of the State as the ultimate duty bearer to protect women and girls from violence, its causes and consequences. . . . Given the systemic, widespread and pervasive nature of this human rights violation, which is experienced largely by women because they are women, a different set of normative and practical measures to respond to, prevent and ultimately eliminate such violence is crucial.[12]

Interestingly, Manjoo's successor to the office of Special Rapporteur, Dubravka Šimonović, appeared less convinced of the necessity for the adoption of legally binding standards at the global level on violence against women.[13] Writing in 2014, prior to her appointment as Special Rapporteur, Šimonović, a former member of the CEDAW Committee, commented, 'One could question whether the lack of an express provision on violence against women is an inadequacy of the [CEDAW] Convention which requires its revision by amendment or even an Optional Protocol on violence against women'.[14] She proceeded to state, 'So far, the Convention's undisputed application to violence against women as a form of discrimination under the Convention indicates that the system can work as it is'.[15] However, during her time in office, Šimonović nevertheless called for submissions from stakeholders on the question of whether there was a need for a separate legally binding treaty on violence against women with a separate monitoring body.

It is notable that in its response to Šimonović's call for submissions, the CEDAW Committee itself expressed the view that no such treaty was

10 Manjoo and Nadj, op. cit., 343.

11 Manjoo and Nadj, op. cit., 343.

12 Report of the Special Rapporteur on Violence Against Women, its causes and consequences, Rashida Manjoo, UN. Doc. A/HRC/29/27, 10 June 2015, at para. 63.

13 See Šimonović, D., 'Global and Regional Standards on Violence Against Women: The Evolution and Synergy of the CEDAW and Istanbul Conventions' (2014) 36 *Human Rights Quarterly* 590 at 601.

14 Šimonović, op. cit., 601.

15 Šimonović, op. cit., 601.

needed. The Committee stated, 'A new instrument and its new monitoring body would certainly increase the burden of States parties and reinforce the trend of fragmentation'.[16] According to the CEDAW Committee, the interpretation of CEDAW as encompassing violence against women, as contained in General Recommendation No. 19,[17] was sufficient. The Committee noted that General Recommendation No. 19 had been frequently availed of by states parties, the Committee itself and other stakeholders including civil society organisations, and noted that an updated General Recommendation on violence against women was soon to be issued.[18] The CEDAW Committee also stated, 'We should avoid fragmentation of policies and legislation at the UN level. . . . [T]he creation of a new convention is contradictive from a viewpoint of States parties which have urged the Committee to streamline our activities'. Additionally, the Committee referred to advances in the 'mainstreaming of gender in the UN human rights mechanisms especially in other treaty bodies'. The CEDAW Committee also highlighted 'the current economic atmosphere which negatively impacts many parts of the world' and commented, 'While many States parties are struggling in costcutting of social programs/budgets including those for combatting (violence against women), it is not an appropriate time to propose a new convention'.

Rashida Manjoo had however previously commented in startlingly blunt terms on the resistance of the CEDAW Committee to the adoption of a UN treaty on violence against women. In 2015 she stated,

> The lack of political will is significant, but so is the resistance by the CEDAW committee and some UN agencies. It is appalling that a treaty that would comprehensively address the normative gap on a human rights issue that is widespread, pervasive, systemic, systematic, cutting across geographic/race/class boundaries, is resisted by people who should know better.

She went on to state,

> As regards CEDAW, the question for me is: how can a new treaty negatively impact CEDAW? This is a weak argument, as CEDAW does not have any direct relevant provisions. . . . I do not minimise the work of the

16 The response of the CEDAW Committee of 31 May 2016 is available at http://www.ohchr.org/Documents/Issues/Women/SR/Framework/CEDAW.pdf (Office of the High Commissioner for Human Rights).

17 Committee on the Elimination of Discrimination Against Women, General Recommendation No. 19, U.N. Doc. A/47/38 (1992). General Recommendation No. 19 was discussed in Chapter Two.

18 This updated General Recommendation was issued as General Recommendation No. 35 on gender-based violence against women, updating General Recommendation No. 19, CEDAW/C/GC/35 (2017). General Recommendation No. 35 will be discussed further later in Chapter Four.

> Committee and I acknowledge that they have tried to interpret CEDAW to include violence. But when you have a human rights violation that is so pervasive, specificity becomes crucial in addressing the obligations of States.[19]

In light of her previous statements on the matter, Rashida Manjoo's participation in a joint call for states to consider strongly the adoption of legally binding standards at the UN level on violence against women is to be expected. What may be rather more surprising is the fact that this call is very specifically for consideration of the adoption of an Optional Protocol to CEDAW on this issue. It is possible that this may represent a development in Manjoo's views on the matter. It may have been the case that Manjoo would have initially supported a stand-alone UN treaty on violence against women, given that she does not appear to have referred specifically to the possibility of the adoption of an Optional Protocol to CEDAW in the statements which she made during her term as Special Rapporteur. Also, in her comments of 2015 on the matter, she asserts that a new treaty would not impact negatively upon CEDAW, an argument which would not be applicable to the adoption of an Optional Protocol to this instrument. In addition, in her report of May 2014, Manjoo referred to 'time constraints when examining State party reports' as resulting in 'insufficient interrogation concerning the information relating to violence against women, its causes and consequences, and insufficient assessment of responses'.[20] It would seem that this problem would be solved by a stand-alone treaty on violence against women with its own monitoring body, but not by an Optional Protocol to CEDAW, the monitoring of which would fall to the CEDAW Committee, thus placing additional pressure on the time constraints involved.

Nevertheless, Manjoo has now moved to a position of stating, along with Reem Alsalem and Dubravka Šimonović, not only that an Optional Protocol to CEDAW on violence against women may be a potential way forward, but that it would indeed be 'essential' for legally binding standards on this issue to take the form of such an Optional Protocol in order to 'ensure that minimum global standards on women's rights are not further compromised, but are upheld and strengthened'. This potential development in Manjoo's approach may be due to practical considerations. As noted earlier, the CEDAW Committee itself had expressed its opposition to the adoption of a stand-alone UN treaty on violence against women, due to concerns regarding 'fragmentation of policies and legislation at the UN level' and fears that a 'new instrument and its new monitoring body would certainly increase the burden of States

19 Manjoo and Nadj, op. cit., 343.

20 Report of the Special Rapporteur on violence against women, its causes and consequences, Rashida Manjoo, U.N. Doc. A/HRC/26/38, 28 May 2014, at para. 76.

parties and reinforce the trend of fragmentation'. In support of its view, the CEDAW Committee highlighted 'the current economic atmosphere which negatively impacts many parts of the world'. However, it is unlikely that the Committee would view an Optional Protocol to CEDAW on violence against women as carrying the same risk of 'fragmentation' as might a stand-alone treaty on this issue, particularly given the fact that the monitoring of state compliance with such an Optional Protocol would fall within the remit of the CEDAW Committee. The Committee may thus be more likely to support the adoption of an Optional Protocol to CEDAW. Nevertheless, it is notable that the Committee has expressed the opinion that the current approach of simply interpreting CEDAW as encompassing violence against women is sufficient in itself without steps being taken as regards the adoption of legally binding standards on this issue. Accordingly, it is by no means certain that the CEDAW Committee would now support even the adoption of an Optional Protocol to CEDAW on violence against women; and it would seem that the support of this Committee would be important in bringing about this development. Indeed, it is very likely that the adoption of legally binding provisions at the UN level on violence against women would only be feasible with the support of the CEDAW Committee, given the importance of the role held by this body in the protection of the rights of women internationally.

Dubravka Šimonović's views on the issue also seem to have developed. As noted previously, in 2014, Šimonović questioned whether the omission from CEDAW of an express provision on violence against women was a matter which needed to be addressed, and expressed the opinion that 'the system can work as it is'.[21] Such a position is in distinct contrast to the views now expressed by Šimonović, along with Manjoo and Reem Alsalem, that 'a global treaty dedicated to ending gender-based violence against women would constitute a timely and effective way of advancing gender equality and non-discrimination, ending violence and achieving greater accountability and justice for crimes committed against women and girls', and that

> history has shown that the lack of a universally accepted legal framework that explicitly defines and spells out the various forms of violence against women, criminalizes it, sets out prevention and protection measures and entitles victims to reparations, continues to be a principal stumbling block that must be overcome.

Nonetheless, it is unlikely that Šimonović would have moved from a position of believing that no legally binding standards at the UN level were necessary to a belief that a stand-alone treaty on violence against violence is needed. It is possible that the rather less radical alternative of an Optional Protocol to

21 Šimonović, op. cit., 601.

CEDAW on violence against women represents somewhat of a compromise position between the initial views of Manjoo and Šimonović respectively. It is also noteworthy that Šimonović is a former member of the CEDAW Committee. Although previously of the view that 'the system can work as it is',[22] Šimonović is now supportive of an Optional Protocol on violence against women, and it is possible that the views of the CEDAW Committee may also develop in such a manner. It is however very unlikely, given its previously expressed views on the matter, that the Committee would move to a position of supporting the adoption of a stand-alone global treaty on violence against women.

In any event, in terms of advancing the debate on the need for the adoption of legally binding standards at the global level on violence against women, it is advantageous that the current UN Special Rapporteur on violence against women, along with two former Special Rapporteurs, have not only agreed upon the need for the adoption of such provisions, but have also adopted an agreed position on the form which such legally binding standards should take. Although it is arguable that the adoption of an Optional Protocol to CEDAW would not be the most effective method to employ, as will be discussed in Chapter Five, nevertheless the fact that the current and former Special Rapporteurs are presenting a unified front on this issue may well serve to advance the chances of legally binding standards being adopted.

The Merits of an Optional Protocol to CEDAW on Violence Against Women

The adoption of an Optional Protocol to CEDAW on violence against women to be monitored by the CEDAW Committee certainly has notable attractions, in that this course of action would be likely to be substantially less costly than the adoption of a stand-alone UN treaty and the establishment of a separate monitoring body. As noted earlier, in 2016, in expressing its opposition to a stand-alone treaty, the CEDAW Committee referred to 'the current economic atmosphere which negatively impacts many parts of the world', and a similar economic reality still exists around the globe today. Also, CEDAW is one of the most widely ratified international treaties, with currently 189 states parties. The fact that states generally are very familiar with CEDAW may encourage them to ratify an Optional Protocol to this instrument, whereas they may perhaps be less likely to ratify a stand-alone treaty on violence against women.

Furthermore, whilst the CEDAW Committee stated that a stand-alone UN treaty 'would certainly increase the burden of States parties', an Optional Protocol to CEDAW would carry less of a reporting burden for states, in that

22 Šimonović, op. cit., 601.

states parties to such a Protocol could include information on compliance within their reports to the CEDAW Committee on compliance with CEDAW more generally. This may in turn have the advantage of encouraging more states to ratify such an instrument. From the perspective of states parties to the UN human rights treaties, it is undeniable that the reporting requirements are time-consuming and costly. If a state is party to a number of such instruments and is required to provide a report on compliance to each of the relevant treaty monitoring bodies every four years, this constitutes a substantial obligation. This may raise the question of whether states should therefore be placed under greater pressure in this regard by the addition of yet another treaty in respect of which reports on compliance must be provided.

If a stand-alone UN treaty on violence against women were to be adopted, questions would also be raised as to how the obligations to be undertaken by states under such an instrument would relate to the work of the CEDAW Committee on this issue. States include information on the steps which they take to combat violence against women in the reports which they submit to the CEDAW Committee, which in turn makes recommendations on this issue in its Concluding Observations on these reports. If a state ratified a stand-alone UN treaty on violence against women, would the state be obliged to provide information on this issue to a new treaty monitoring body and also, perhaps in a less detailed format, to the CEDAW Committee? Conversely, if such an instrument were to be adopted by the UN, would this encourage states which chose not to ratify it but which were parties to CEDAW to argue that they should not be subject to scrutiny by the CEDAW Committee on the issue of violence against women as they have chosen not to ratify the UN treaty on this matter? It is arguable that the CEDAW Committee may have been correct in its assessment that 'A new instrument and its new monitoring body would certainly . . . reinforce the trend of fragmentation'.

It must also be remembered that although there is currently no UN treaty on violence against women, there are treaties specifically on this issue within three of the regional human rights systems – the Convention of Belém do Pará within the Inter-American system, the Istanbul Convention in the context of the Council of Europe and the Convention on Ending Violence Against Women and Girls within the African Union. The Istanbul Convention is particularly detailed in terms of the obligations which it places on states, and therefore for states which are already parties to this Convention in particular, ratification of a global treaty on violence against women would amount to duplication of obligations to a substantial degree. This in itself would of course be unproblematic – if a state has similar or even identical obligations under two treaties, compliance with one will therefore mean compliance with the other. However, the primary monitoring mechanism under the Istanbul Convention is, yet again, a reporting procedure. If a state were able to submit the same report to the 'Group of experts on action against violence against women and domestic violence' (also known as 'GREVIO'), which is one of the monitoring bodies under the Istanbul Convention, and to a new treaty monitoring body on violence against women, no difficulty would arise. Nevertheless, it is extremely unlikely that this would be the case. The reporting procedure under the Istanbul Convention requires states parties, after their initial report, to focus each of their subsequent periodic reports on a particular aspect of violence against women as decided in advance of each round of reporting by GREVIO.[23] A new UN treaty body may require states to report on all aspects of compliance. Alternatively, even if a similar approach were taken to that adopted by GREVIO, it is unlikely that there would be sufficient coordination between GREVIO and a new UN treaty monitoring body to ensure that the same aspect of violence against women would be adopted for consideration by both bodies simultaneously for each round of reporting, in order to allow states which are parties to both instruments to submit very similar reports to both monitoring bodies. Indeed, it is debatable whether the level of coordination which such a system would entail would be viewed as desirable by either GREVIO or a new UN treaty body on violence against women.

The Possible Content of an Optional Protocol to CEDAW on Violence Against Women

It is likely that the substantive content of an Optional Protocol to CEDAW on violence against women would be based largely on the CEDAW Committee's General Recommendation No. 35 on gender-based violence.[24] The existence of this General Recommendation would mean that there would be an initial blueprint from which to work in terms of drafting such an Optional Protocol. The fact that the CEDAW Committee already refers to General Recommendation No. 35 when assessing state compliance with CEDAW may encourage states to ratify an Optional Protocol based on this General Recommendation, given that they would already have a level of familiarity with the provisions contained therein. As it is likely that an Optional Protocol would be based largely on General Recommendation No. 35, the chapter will proceed to analyse the content of this General Recommendation.[25]

The CEDAW Committee adopted its General Recommendation No. 35 in July 2017 with the purpose of updating the Committee's General Recommendation No. 19 on violence against women, which had been issued 25 years previously. While the title of General Recommendation No. 19 referred

23 See Article 68 of the Istanbul Convention. Further discussion of the monitoring procedures under the Istanbul Convention can be found in Chapter Five.

24 Committee on the Elimination of Discrimination Against Women, General Recommendation No. 35 on gender-based violence against women, updating General Recommendation No. 19, CEDAW/C/GC/35 (2017).

25 Discussion of General Recommendation No. 35 can also be found in McQuigg, R., 'The CEDAW Committee and Gender-Based Violence Against Women: General Recommendation No. 35' (2017) 6 *International Human Rights Law Review* 263.

simply to 'violence against women', interestingly the title of General Recommendation No. 35 instead uses the phrase 'gender-based violence against women'. According to the CEDAW Committee, this more specific term is used as it 'makes explicit the gendered causes and impacts of the violence'.[26] It seems that the CEDAW Committee decided to use this term from the outset in order to counter arguments which advocate a gender-neutral approach to addressing violence. Notably such gender-neutral approaches had received strong criticism from former UN Special Rapporteur on violence against women, Rashida Manjoo. In 2015, Manjoo had commented,

> The distortion of understanding of equality and gendered responses, is leading to gender-neutral responses and an abandonment of a focus on women's empowerment. International human rights law demands substantive equality, not formal equality. Unfortunately we see a move towards neutrality and consequently towards formal equality, under the guise of equality. This is a challenge facing the developing world but also the developed world. Countries that have not even started the hard work of redress for harms suffered by women, have found it an easy way out by adopting this approach . . . the goal of substantive equality will be difficult to attain in a context of growing gender neutrality in laws, policies and practices.[27]

With the use of the phrase 'gender-based violence against women', the CEDAW Committee emphasises that the issue in question is essentially violence directed at women because they are women, thus making this type of violence different from violence more generally and thereby justifying and indeed necessitating a gendered response. As the Committee states, 'gender-based violence against women is one of the fundamental social, political and economic means by which the subordinate position of women with respect to men and their stereotyped roles are perpetuated'.[28] Indeed General Recommendation No. 35 proceeds to state,

> The Committee regards gender-based violence against women to be rooted in gender-related factors such as the ideology of men's entitlement and privilege over women, social norms regarding masculinity, the need to assert male control or power, enforce gender roles, or prevent, discourage or punish what is considered to be unacceptable female behavior. These factors also contribute to the explicit or implicit social acceptance of gender-based violence against women, often still considered as a private matter, and to the widespread impunity for it.[29]

26 General Recommendation No. 35, at para. 9.
27 Manjoo and Nadj, op. cit., 338–339.
28 General Recommendation No. 35, at para. 10.
29 General Recommendation No. 35, at para. 19.

Notably the effects of gender-based violence against women are explained in considerably more detail by the CEDAW Committee in General Recommendation No. 35 than they were in General Recommendation No. 19, which on this point simply stated, 'Gender-based violence is a form of discrimination that seriously inhibits women's ability to enjoy rights and freedoms on a basis of equality with men'.[30] It seems that the much more detailed explanation found in General Recommendation No. 35 is certainly to be welcomed. At a time when there is a move towards gender-neutral approaches, General Recommendation No. 35 provides a timely reminder of the reasons that gender-based violence against women requires a gendered response.

In General Recommendation No. 19, the CEDAW Committee made the point that 'Gender-based violence may breach specific provisions of the Convention, regardless of whether those provisions expressly mention violence'.[31] However, General Recommendation No. 35 goes considerably further and states, 'Gender-based violence against women constitutes discrimination against women under Article 1 and therefore engages all of the obligations in the Convention'.[32] While a large part of General Recommendation No. 19 was devoted to a section entitled 'Comments on specific articles of the Convention', which explained how a selection of CEDAW provisions related to violence against women, this is not the approach adopted in General Recommendation No. 35. Although specific provisions of CEDAW are referred to in the latter, overall there appears to be less of an emphasis on explaining how precisely the specific provisions of CEDAW mandate the obligations and recommendations put forward by the CEDAW Committee. This broader approach may be problematic, as will be discussed later in this chapter.

The primary difference between General Recommendation Nos. 19 and 35 relates to the amount of detail contained therein on the responsibilities of states parties. For example, many acts of gender-based violence are committed by private individuals, which means that the concept of 'due diligence' is of particular importance in this area. In General Recommendation No. 19, the CEDAW Committee asserted, 'Under general international law and specific human rights covenants, States may also be responsible for private acts if they fail to act with due diligence to prevent violations of rights or to investigate and punish acts of violence, and for providing compensation'.[33] General Recommendation No. 35 sets out in considerably more detail what the concept

30 General Recommendation No. 19, at para. 1.

31 General Recommendation No. 19, at para. 6.

32 General Recommendation No. 35, at para. 21. Article 1 of CEDAW states, 'For the purposes of the present Convention, the term "discrimination against women" shall mean any distinction, exclusion or restriction made on the basis of sex which has the effect or purpose of impairing or nullifying the recognition, enjoyment or exercise by women, irrespective of their marital status, on a basis of equality of men and women, of human rights and fundamental freedoms in the political, economic, social, cultural, civil or any other field.'

33 General Recommendation No. 19, at para. 9.

of due diligence actually entails in practice. It specifies that this obligation encompasses actions by corporations operating extraterritorially, and that states parties must adopt measures to prevent human rights breaches abroad by corporations over which they may exercise influence, whether by using incentives or by regulatory means. The General Recommendation continues,

> Under the obligation of due diligence, States parties have to adopt and implement diverse measures to tackle gender-based violence against women committed by non-State actors. They are required to have laws, institutions and a system in place to address such violence. Also, States parties are obliged to ensure that these function effectively in practice, and are supported and diligently enforced by all State agents and bodies.[34]

As regards the more specific recommendations made by the CEDAW Committee, again these are set out in substantially greater detail in General Recommendation No. 35 than in General Recommendation No. 19. For example, in relation to legislative measures, General Recommendation No. 19 stated, 'States parties should ensure that laws against family violence and abuse, rape, sexual assault and other gender-based violence give adequate protection to all women, and respect their integrity and dignity'.[35] However, General Recommendation No. 35 contains an entire section entitled 'General Legislative Measures' which consists of five paragraphs,[36] the first of which asserts that states should

> Ensure that all forms of gender-based violence against women in all spheres, which amount to a violation of their physical, sexual, or psychological identity, are criminalised and introduce, without delay, or strengthen legal sanctions commensurate with the gravity of the offence as well as civil remedies.[37]

General Recommendation No. 35 also asserts that states should ensure that all legal systems protect victims/survivors of gender-based violence against women and ensure they have access to justice and to an effective remedy;[38] and lists in detail types of legal provisions which are discriminatory against women and should therefore be repealed.[39] In addition, states should examine

34 General Recommendation No. 35, at para. 24(b).
35 General Recommendation No. 19, at para. 24(b).
36 General Recommendation No. 35, at paras. 29–33.
37 General Recommendation No. 35, at para. 29.
38 General Recommendation No. 35, at para. 30.
39 General Recommendation No. 35, at para. 31.

gender-neutral laws and policies to ensure that they do not create or perpetuate inequality, and amend or repeal them if they are found to do so;[40] ensure that sexual assault is characterised as a crime against women's right to personal security and their physical, sexual and psychological integrity; ensure that the definition of sexual crimes is based on lack of freely given consent; and ensure that any time limitations prioritise the interests of victims/survivors and afford consideration to circumstances hindering their capacity to report violence to the authorities.[41]

In relation to the need to raise awareness in society of the issues involved in violence against women, General Recommendation No. 19 required states parties to 'identify the nature and extent of attitudes, customs and practices that perpetuate violence against women, and the kinds of violence that result' in their periodic reports to the CEDAW Committee.[42] States should adopt effective measures to overcome such attitudes and practices, and report on the effect of such measures.[43] It was also recommended that states parties 'introduce education and public information programmes to help eliminate prejudices which hinder women's equality'.[44] Again General Recommendation No. 35 sets out in much greater detail the measures which states parties should adopt in this respect. It is recommended that states parties adopt and implement

> appropriate preventive measures to address the underlying causes of gender-based violence against women, including patriarchal attitudes and stereotypes, inequality in the family and the neglect or denial of women's civil, political, economic, social and cultural rights, as well as to promote women's empowerment, agency and voice.[45]

States parties should also

> Develop and implement effective measures, with the active participation of all relevant stakeholders, such as women's organisations and those representing marginalised groups of women and girls, to address and eradicate the stereotypes, prejudices, customs and practices . . . that condone or promote gender-based violence against women and underpin structural inequality of women with men.[46]

40 General Recommendation No. 35, at para. 32.
41 General Recommendation No. 35, at para. 33.
42 General Recommendation No. 19, at para. 24(e).
43 General Recommendation No. 19, at para. 24(e) and (f).
44 General Recommendation No.19, at para. 24(f).
45 General Recommendation No. 35, at para. 34.
46 General Recommendation No. 35, at para. 35.

It is recommended that these measures include the integration of gender equality content into curricula at all levels of education. In addition, General Recommendation No. 35 provides detail on the nature of the awareness-raising programmes which should be implemented. General Recommendation No. 19 had stated, 'Gender-sensitive training of judicial and law enforcement officers and other public officials is essential for the effective implementation of the Convention'.[47] However, General Recommendation No. 35 states, 'Mandatory, recurrent and effective capacity-building, education and training' as regards violence against women should be provided for judges, lawyers, law enforcement officers, health-care professionals, and education, social and welfare personnel; and detail is included on aspects which should be encompassed by such training.[48]

As regards the involvement of the media, General Recommendation No. 19 required 'Effective measures . . . be taken to ensure that the media respect and promote respect for women'.[49] General Recommendation No. 35 expands upon this by recommending that states parties

> Adopt and implement effective measures to encourage all media, including advertising and information and communication technologies to eliminate discrimination against women in their activity, including harmful and stereotyped portrayal of women or specific groups of women, such as women human rights defenders.[50]

It is stated that such measures should encompass encouraging the creation or strengthening of self-regulatory mechanisms by the media aimed at eliminating gender stereotypes and at addressing gender-based violence against women that takes place through their platforms and services;[51] the issuing of guidelines for appropriate media coverage of cases involving gender-based violence against women;[52] and the establishment or strengthening the capacity of national human rights institutions to monitor or consider complaints regarding any media that portray images that are gender-discriminatory or content that demeans or objectifies women.[53]

In relation to violence in the workplace, General Recommendation No. 19 stated simply, 'States parties should include in their reports information on sexual harassment, and on measures to protect women from sexual

47 General Recommendation No. 19, at para. 24(b).
48 General Recommendation No. 35, at para. 38.
49 General Recommendation No. 19, at para. 24(d).
50 General Recommendation No. 35, at para. 37.
51 General Recommendation No. 35, at para. 37(a).
52 General Recommendation No. 35, at para. 37(b).
53 General Recommendation No. 35, at para. 37(c).

harassment and other forms of violence or coercion in the workplace'.[54] Again General Recommendation No. 35 goes much further and asserts that states parties should

> Encourage, also through the use of incentives and corporate responsibility models, the engagement of the private sector, including businesses and transnational corporations, in efforts to eradicate all forms of gender-based violence against women, and to enhance its responsibility for such violence in the scope of its action. This should entail protocols and procedures addressing all forms of gender-based violence that may occur in the workplace or affect women workers, including effective and accessible internal complaints procedures that do not exclude recourse to law enforcement authorities. This should also address workplace entitlements for women victims/survivors of such violence.[55]

As regards the provision of support measures to victims/survivors of violence against women, General Recommendation No. 19 asserted, 'States parties should establish or support services for victims of family violence, rape, sex assault and other forms of gender-based violence, including refuges, specially trained health workers, rehabilitation and counselling'.[56] It was also provided, 'Measures that are necessary to overcome family violence should include . . . services to ensure the safety and security of victims of family violence, including refuges, counselling and rehabilitation programmes'.[57] Much more detail is provided in General Recommendation No. 35, which refers to

> Ensuring access to financial aid and free or low-cost high quality legal aid, medical, psychosocial and counselling services, education, affordable housing, land, child care, training and employment opportunities for women victims/survivors and their family members. . . . States should provide specialist women's support services such as free of charge 24-hour helplines, and sufficient numbers of safe and adequately equipped crisis, support and referral centres, as well as adequate shelters for women, their children, and other family members as required.[58]

General Recommendation No. 35 also asserts that states parties should provide support measures as regards gender-based violence to women in

54 General Recommendation No. 19, at para. 24(j).
55 General Recommendation No. 35, at para. 39.
56 General Recommendation No. 19, at para. 24(k).
57 General Recommendation No. 19, at para. 24(r).
58 General Recommendation No. 35, at para. 40(c).

institutions, such as asylum centres;[59] and establish and implement appropriate multi-sectorial referral mechanisms to ensure effective access of women survivors to comprehensive services.[60]

In relation to criminal and civil law measures of protection, General Recommendation No. 19 set out,

> States parties should take all legal and other measures that are necessary to provide effective protection of women against gender-based violence, including, inter alia, effective legal measures, including penal sanctions, civil remedies compensatory provisions to protect women against all kinds of violence, including, inter alia, violence and abuse in the family, sexual assault and sexual harassment in the workplace.[61]

It also stated, 'Measures that are necessary to overcome family violence should include criminal penalties where necessary and civil remedies in cases of domestic violence'.[62] General Recommendation No. 35 asserts that states parties should

> Ensure effective access of victims to courts and tribunals; ensure authorities adequately respond to all cases of gender-based violence against women, including by applying criminal law and as appropriate ex officio prosecution to bring the alleged perpetrators to trial in a fair, impartial, timely and expeditious manner and imposing adequate penalties. Fees or court charges should not be imposed on victims/survivors.[63]

The General Recommendation also emphasises that gender-based violence against women should not be mandatorily referred to alternative dispute resolution procedures, and sets out guidance on such procedures if they are used.[64] In addition, states should adopt effective measures to protect and assist women complainants and witnesses of gender-based violence before, during and after legal proceedings.[65] As regards civil measures of protection, there should be 'immediate risk assessment and protection, comprising a wide range of effective measures and, where appropriate, the issuance and monitoring of

59 General Recommendation No. 35, at para. 40(d).
60 General Recommendation No. 35, at para. 40(e).
61 General Recommendation No. 19, at para. 24(t).
62 General Recommendation No. 19, at para. 24(r).
63 General Recommendation No. 35, at para. 44.
64 General Recommendation No. 35, at para. 45.
65 General Recommendation No. 35, at para. 40(a).

eviction, protection, restraining or emergency barring orders against alleged perpetrators'.[66] The General Recommendation also states,

> Perpetrators or alleged perpetrators' rights or claims during and after judicial proceedings, including with respect to property, privacy, child custody, access, contact and visitation, should be determined in the light of women's and children's human rights to life and physical, sexual and psychological integrity, and guided by the principle of the best interests of the child.[67]

All legal proceedings should respect and strengthen the autonomy of victims/survivors of gender-based violence.[68]

As regards research and data collection on violence against women, General Recommendation No. 19 simply asserted, 'States parties should encourage the compilation of statistics and research on the extent, causes and effects of violence, and on the effectiveness of measures to prevent and deal with violence'.[69] Again General Recommendation No. 35 goes much further than this and includes four paragraphs on what data should be collected and the procedure for collecting such information.[70]

In terms of the provision of reparation to victims/survivors of violence against women, the only reference to this issue in General Recommendation No. 19 was that 'Effective complaints procedures and remedies, including compensation, should be provided'.[71] General Recommendation No. 35 includes much more detail on this issue. In addition to asserting that states parties should provide effective reparation to victims/survivors,

> Reparation should include different measures, such as monetary compensation and the provision of legal, social and health services including sexual, reproductive and mental health for a complete recovery, and satisfaction and guarantees of non-repetition. . . . Such reparations should be adequate, promptly attributed, holistic and proportionate to the gravity of the harm suffered.[72]

It is also recommended that states parties establish reparation funds for gender-based violence against women, and detail is provided as regards how reparation programmes should be implemented.[73]

66 General Recommendation No. 35, at para. 40(b).
67 General Recommendation No. 35, at para. 40(b).
68 General Recommendation No. 35, at para. 41
69 General Recommendation No. 19, at para. 24(c).
70 General Recommendation No. 35, at paras. 49–52.
71 General Recommendation No. 19, at para. 24(i).
72 General Recommendation No. 35, at para. 46.
73 General Recommendation No. 35, at para. 47.

In addition, there are a number of areas mentioned in General Recommendation No. 35 which were not referred to in General Recommendation No. 19. For example, General Recommendation No. 35 advises that states parties

> Develop and implement effective measures to make public spaces safe and accessible to all women and girls, including by promoting and supporting community-based measures adopted with participation of women's groups. These measures should include ensuring adequate physical infrastructure, including lighting, in urban and rural settings, particularly in and around schools.[74]

It is also recommended that states parties address factors such as accessibility and availability of firearms and of substances such as acid which may be used to attack women.[75] In addition, states parties should 'Develop and evaluate all legislation, policies and programmes in consultation with civil society organisations, in particular women's organisations, including those that represent women who experience intersecting forms of discrimination'.[76] General Recommendation No. 35 also asserts that states parties should allocate appropriate financial and human resources to implement effectively laws and policies surrounding gender-based violence against women, including the provision of support to women's organisations.[77] States should seek support, where necessary, from external sources such as UN specialised agencies as regards designing and implementing appropriate measures to address gender-based violence against women.[78]

Overall, General Recommendation No. 35 contains detailed advice to states parties to CEDAW on how they should address the issue of violence against women. Generally speaking, this advice is not new. As was discussed in Chapter Two, the UN has issued a multitude of documents relevant to this issue. For example, the UN General Assembly has adopted various Resolutions in this area, including the UN Declaration on the Elimination of Violence Against Women.[79] Resolutions as regards violence against women were

74 General Recommendation No. 35, at para. 36.
75 General Recommendation No. 35, at para. 43.
76 General Recommendation No. 35, at para. 48.
77 General Recommendation No. 35, at para. 53.
78 General Recommendation No. 35, at para. 54.
79 General Assembly Resolution A/RES/48/104, 20 December 1993. See also for example, the Resolutions of the General Assembly on intensification of efforts to eliminate all forms of violence against women which were adopted on 19 December 2006 (A/RES/61/143); 18 December 2007 (A/RES/62/133); 18 December 2008 (A/RES/63/155); 18 December 2009 (A/RES/64/137); 21 December 2010 (A/RES/65/187); and 20 December 2012 (A/RES/67/144).

also adopted by the Commission on Human Rights[80] and have been adopted by the Human Rights Council.[81] In addition, violence against women was addressed in the Vienna Declaration and Programme of Action which was adopted by the World Conference on Human Rights in Vienna in June 1993. Since the creation of the office of the UN Special Rapporteur on violence against women in 1994, those who have held this post have issued numerous reports. Additionally, the Beijing Declaration and Platform for Action, which was issued following the Fourth World Conference on Women organised by the UN and which took place in 1995, contains various recommendations on the measures that states should adopt to address violence against women.[82] The CEDAW Committee itself has issued a huge number of Concluding Observations relevant to this issue in relation to the periodic reports submitted by states parties, and has also made recommendations to states parties in dealing with communications submitted under the individual complaints procedure found in the Optional Protocol to CEDAW. In effect, General Recommendation No. 35 distils the key elements of the statements on violence against women which the CEDAW Committee in particular had previously made and puts these into one document.

General Recommendation No. 35 was of course a very positive addition to this canon of material. Having the key recommendations made by the CEDAW Committee (and indeed the UN human rights bodies more generally) in one document makes this information much more accessible, not only to states, but also to civil society groups working in the area of combating violence against women. General Recommendation No. 35 constitutes a very useful document which such groups can use in order to place pressure on states to adopt further measures to address this issue. It is also advantageous that a large number of civil society groups had an input into the drafting process of General Recommendation No. 35 through making submissions to the CEDAW Committee on a draft version of the General Recommendation.[83] General Recommendation No. 35 covers most, if not all, of what any

80 See for example Commission on Human Rights Resolution E/CN.4/RES/2001/49, 23 April 2001; Commission on Human Rights Resolution E/CN.4/RES/2004/46, 20 April 2004.

81 See for example Resolution 7/24 (2008) 'Elimination of Violence Against Women'; Resolution 11/2 (2009) 'Accelerating Efforts to Eliminate All Forms of Violence Against Women'; Resolution 14/12 (2010) 'Accelerating Efforts to Eliminate All Forms of Violence Against Women: Ensuring Due Diligence in Prevention'; Resolution 20/12 (2012) 'Accelerating Efforts to Eliminate All Forms of Violence Against Women: Remedies for Women Who Have Been Subjected to Violence'.

82 Beijing Platform for Action, U.N. Doc. A/CONF. 177/20 (1995).

83 In July 2016 the CEDAW Committee decided to issue a draft update of General Recommendation No. 19 and invite all interested parties to submit comments in writing on this draft by September 2016. The final version of the draft update was issued in July 2017 as General Recommendation No. 35.

Optional Protocol to CEDAW on violence against women would be likely to include, and the existence of this General Recommendation would provide considerable assistance to the drafting process of a potential Optional Protocol on this issue.

Conclusion

In conclusion, as was analysed in this chapter, the first potential form which could be taken by legally binding standards at the UN level on violence against women is an Optional Protocol to CEDAW on this issue. As was discussed earlier, the current UN Special Rapporteur on violence against women, its causes and consequences, Reem Alsalem, along with two previous holders of this mandate, Dubravka Šimonović and Rashida Manjoo, have issued a joint call for states to consider strongly the adoption of such an Optional Protocol. In terms of advancing the debate on the need for the adoption of legally binding standards at the global level on violence against women, it is advantageous that the current UN Special Rapporteur on violence against women, along with two former Special Rapporteurs, have adopted an agreed position on the form which such legally binding standards should take. The fact that the current and former Special Rapporteurs are presenting a unified front on this issue may well serve to advance the chances of legally binding standards being adopted.

As was discussed in this chapter, the adoption of an Optional Protocol to CEDAW on violence against women to be monitored by the CEDAW Committee certainly has notable attractions, as this course of action would be likely to be substantially less costly than the adoption of a stand-alone treaty and the establishment of a separate monitoring body. Also, this approach would carry less of a reporting burden for states. It is likely that the substantive content of an Optional Protocol to CEDAW on violence against women would be based largely on the CEDAW Committee's General Recommendation No. 35 on gender-based violence. The existence of this General Recommendation would mean that there would be an initial blueprint from which to work in terms of drafting such an Optional Protocol. The fact that the CEDAW Committee already refers to General Recommendation No. 35 when assessing state compliance with CEDAW may encourage states to ratify an Optional Protocol based on this General Recommendation, given that they would already have a level of familiarity with the provisions contained therein. As was examined in this chapter, General Recommendation No. 35 covers most, if not all, of what any Optional Protocol to CEDAW on violence against women would be likely to include, and the existence of this General Recommendation would provide considerable assistance to the drafting process of a potential Optional Protocol on this issue.

However, the adoption of an Optional Protocol to CEDAW, as opposed to a stand-alone treaty, could also carry significant disadvantages. For example, the CEDAW Committee already works under considerable pressure, and it is difficult to see how this body could undertake any additional burden of monitoring. It is arguable that the adoption of an Optional Protocol to CEDAW would not be the most effective method of achieving the goal of implementing legally binding standards at the global level on violence against women. Chapter Five will therefore proceed to examine another form which legally binding provisions at the UN level on this issue could take, namely a stand-alone treaty on violence against women.

5 A Stand-Alone UN Treaty on Violence Against Women

Chapter Five examines another form which legally binding provisions at the UN level on violence against women could take, namely a stand-alone UN treaty on this issue. By contrast to an Optional Protocol to CEDAW, as was discussed in Chapter Four, the adoption of a stand-alone UN treaty on violence against women with its own monitoring body would allow for much more detailed scrutiny of state responses to this issue. This point is brought into particularly sharp focus through an examination of the monitoring work which is being carried out in relation to the Istanbul Convention. Essentially the adoption of a stand-alone UN treaty on violence against women with its own monitoring body would allow greater scope for in-depth evaluation of state compliance and for the incorporation of innovative variations on the traditional reporting procedure.

The Merits of a Stand-Alone UN Treaty on Violence Against Women

As was explored in Chapter Four, using the method of the adoption of an Optional Protocol to CEDAW to put in place legally binding standards at the UN level on violence against women would have significant merits. For example, this course of action would be likely to be substantially less costly than the adoption of a stand-alone UN treaty and the establishment of a separate monitoring body. Also, an Optional Protocol to CEDAW would carry less of a reporting burden for states, in that states parties to such a Protocol could include information on compliance within their reports to the CEDAW Committee on compliance with CEDAW more generally. This may in turn have the advantage of encouraging more states to ratify such an instrument.

As was also discussed in Chapter Four, in December 2023, the current UN Special Rapporteur on violence against women, its causes and consequences, Reem Alsalem, along with two previous holders of this role, Dubravka Šimonović and Rashida Manjoo, issued a joint call for states to consider strongly the adoption of an Optional Protocol to CEDAW on violence against

DOI: 10.4324/9781003603689-5

women.[1] This statement emphasised the need for legally binding provisions on this issue to be put in place at the global level, and asserted, 'To ensure that minimum global standards on women's rights are not further compromised, but are upheld and strengthened, it would be essential for this global treaty to be attached to CEDAW as an optional protocol'. The statement, though, did not elaborate further on the reasons that the current and former Special Rapporteurs were of the view that it was necessary for such legally binding provisions to take the form of an Optional Protocol to CEDAW, as opposed to a stand-alone UN treaty on violence against women. Indeed, the justification put forward for this view – that is, 'To ensure that minimum global standards on women's rights are not further compromised, but are upheld and strengthened' – could be said to be somewhat vague. Presumably, the phrase 'minimum global standards on women's rights' was intended as a reference to CEDAW and the work of the CEDAW Committee, which is of course extremely important. However, it is not entirely clear why the creation of a stand-alone treaty on violence against women would risk compromising such global standards on the rights of women. Indeed Rashida Manjoo commented in 2015, 'As regards CEDAW, the question for me is: how can a new treaty negatively impact CEDAW? This is a weak argument, as CEDAW does not have any direct relevant provisions'.[2]

It is possible that the decision of the current and former Special Rapporteurs to support the format of an Optional Protocol to CEDAW for legally binding provisions at the UN level on violence against women may have been due, at least partly, to political considerations, rather than necessarily to a belief that the vehicle of an Optional Protocol would be the best way of achieving the optimal level of effectiveness of such provisions. As was discussed in Chapter Four, the CEDAW Committee has expressed the view that the current approach of interpreting CEDAW in such a manner so as to encompass violence against women is sufficient, which seems to indicate that this Committee may not support the adoption of legally binding provisions in any format, including that of an Optional Protocol to CEDAW. Nevertheless, the Committee has stated in particular, 'A new instrument and its new monitoring body would certainly increase the burden of States parties and reinforce the trend of fragmentation',[3] and has highlighted the cost implica-

1 Statement by current and former Special Rapporteurs on violence against women, its causes and consequences, 'Now Is the Time for an Optional Protocol to CEDAW on Violence Against Women and Girls', 7 December 2023, available at https://www.ohchr.org/sites/default/files/documents/issues/women/sr/statements/stm-op-vaw-sr-vaw-7-12-23.pdf.

2 Manjoo, R. and Nadj, D., '"Bridging the Divide": An Interview With Professor Rashida Manjoo, UN Special Rapporteur on Violence Against Women' (2015) 23 *Feminist Legal Studies* 329 at 343.

3 See http://www.ohchr.org/Documents/Issues/Women/SR/Framework/CEDAW.pdf, 31 May 2016, Office of the High Commissioner for Human Rights.

tions of a new convention. A proposal to adopt a new stand-alone treaty on violence against women would not therefore enjoy the support of the CEDAW Committee. However, it is possible that the support of the Committee may be obtained for the adoption of an Optional Protocol to CEDAW on violence against women. For example, Dubravka Šimonović is a former member of the CEDAW Committee who, writing in 2014, questioned whether the omission from CEDAW of an express provision on violence against women was a matter which needed to be addressed, and expressed the view that 'the system can work as it is'.[4] Šimonović has nevertheless now joined with Rashida Manjoo and Reem Alsalem to call for states to consider strongly the adoption of an Optional Protocol to CEDAW on violence against women, and is in agreement with them that 'Now is the time for an optional protocol to CEDAW on violence against women and girls'. It is very possible that the current members of the CEDAW Committee may likewise now adopt a similar viewpoint. Without the support of the CEDAW Committee, any attempt to adopt legally binding standards at the UN level on violence against women would almost certainly be doomed to failure, given the very important role which this Committee plays internationally in the protection of the rights of women. Indeed, it is very unlikely that states could be persuaded to ratify an instrument containing legally binding provisions on violence against women if such an instrument did not enjoy the support of the CEDAW Committee.

Given that the current and former UN Special Rapporteurs on violence against women have now expressed their support for an Optional Protocol to CEDAW on violence against women, it is of course now very unlikely that the more radical alternative of a stand-alone UN treaty on this issue would be adopted. Nevertheless, the adoption of an Optional Protocol to CEDAW, as opposed to a stand-alone treaty, could carry significant disadvantages. It is certainly true that the CEDAW Committee does make valiant attempts to address the issue of violence against women. As was discussed in Chapter Two, the Committee regularly makes recommendations to states on this matter in its Concluding Observations on state reports. However, the problem is that violence against women is only one of a multitude of issues which need to be addressed by the CEDAW Committee in relation to each state report which is presented. The Committee works under extreme time pressures and has only a relatively short time to consider each report. This means that the time which can be spent on the consideration of violence against women is very limited, a situation which is particularly problematic given the complex and multi-faceted nature of this issue. Due to the pressures under which the CEDAW Committee works, it is difficult to see how this body could undertake

4 Šimonović, D., 'Global and Regional Standards on Violence Against Women: The Evolution and Synergy of the CEDAW and Istanbul Conventions' (2014) 36 *Human Rights Quarterly* 590 at 601.

any additional burden of monitoring. By contrast, a treaty monitoring body focused solely on the issue of violence against women would be able to assess compliance in a more detailed manner than would the CEDAW Committee, the capacity of which is already over-stretched.

In addition, given that the CEDAW Committee currently refers to General Recommendation No. 35 in its Concluding Observations on state reports, it could be that the adoption of an Optional Protocol on violence against women would make little difference in practice, as the CEDAW Committee may well be unable to devote any additional time to monitoring state responses to violence against women in any greater depth than it does currently. As was discussed in Chapter Four, it is very likely that any Optional Protocol to CEDAW on this issue would be based heavily on General Recommendation No. 35. The rather odd situation could therefore occur whereby states which have chosen not to ratify an Optional Protocol on violence against women could nevertheless be held to account, through the Committee's use of General Recommendation No. 35, as regards compliance with essentially the same obligations as states which have ratified such a Protocol. Alternatively, states which may choose not to ratify an Optional Protocol may seek to argue that the CEDAW Committee should not refer to General Recommendation No. 35 when assessing their compliance with CEDAW, given that they are not party to similar obligations contained in a Protocol. This may lead to a reduction on the part of such states in their attempts to address violence against women.

One of the key advantages of a global treaty on violence against women would be that it would enable the monitoring body of such an instrument to focus in an exclusive and in-depth manner on this particular area and to make detailed recommendations to states on this issue. Although it is probable that states which are parties to both a UN treaty on violence against women and to CEDAW would still be required to include information on their responses to violence against women in their periodic reports to the CEDAW Committee, it is very unlikely that this would constitute any real inconvenience for such states. The fact that states parties to a UN treaty on violence against women would be required to report to a new treaty monitoring body on the measures which they adopt to address this issue in a more detailed manner than they do at present to the CEDAW Committee would be a small price to pay for the benefits which would be afforded by such an instrument. Indeed, it is noteworthy that the CEDAW Committee has regularly urged states within the Council of Europe which are not yet parties to the Istanbul Convention to ratify this instrument, thereby encouraging such states to take on a similar reporting obligation as that which would be entailed by becoming party to a global treaty on violence against women. Essentially the adoption of a stand-alone treaty on this issue with its own monitoring body would allow for much more detailed scrutiny of state responses to violence against women. This point is brought into particularly sharp focus when a comparison is made between monitoring of state compliance with the Istanbul Convention – the Council of Europe's treaty on violence against women – and the monitoring of state responses to violence against women as carried out by the CEDAW Committee.

Monitoring of State Compliance With the Istanbul Convention – A Comparative Analysis

The monitoring mechanisms of the Istanbul Convention are found in Articles 66–70 of this instrument. These provisions set up two bodies – a Group of Experts on Action Against Violence Against Women and Domestic Violence (GREVIO) and a Committee of the Parties. The latter is comprised of representatives of the states parties to the Convention.[5] The members of GREVIO are elected by the Committee of the Parties from among candidates nominated by the states parties.[6] GREVIO is tasked with the responsibility of monitoring the implementation of the provisions of the Convention by states parties,[7] and Article 68 sets out the monitoring procedures to be carried out by GREVIO. The primary monitoring mechanism is a reporting procedure. Under Article 68(1), 'Parties shall submit to the Secretary General of the Council of Europe, based on a questionnaire prepared by GREVIO, a report on legislative and other measures giving effect to the provisions of this Convention'. This report is then considered by GREVIO in conjunction with representatives of the state party concerned. GREVIO adopted its baseline questionnaire in March 2016, and completion of this questionnaire requires states parties to provide detailed information on their compliance with all aspects of the Convention. Non-governmental organisations and civil society groups working in the area of combating violence against women are also invited to submit information on the implementation of the Convention.[8] Under Article 68(3), subsequent evaluation procedures are then divided into rounds, the length of which is to be determined by GREVIO. At the beginning of each round, GREVIO chooses the specific provisions of the Convention on which the evaluation procedure will focus and sends out a questionnaire accordingly. In October 2022, GREVIO adopted the questionnaire for the second evaluation procedure which has the theme of 'building trust by providing support, protection and justice'. This evaluation procedure aims to assess the progress of states parties regarding a selected number of provisions of the Istanbul Convention which set out standards for law enforcement agencies and actors within criminal justice systems, in relation to the provision of support services for victims and

5 Article 67(1) of the Istanbul Convention.
6 Article 66(2).
7 Article 66(1).
8 Article 68(5).

the implementation of a victim-centred approach. Article 68(9) provides for the organisation by GREVIO of country visits if the information obtained is insufficient. Under Article 68(11), based on all the information received, GREVIO adopts a report on the measures taken by the state party in question to implement the provisions of the Convention, which is sent to the state party and to the Committee of the Parties. GREVIO's report is made public, as are eventual comments from the state party concerned. Under Article 68(12), the Committee of the Parties may adopt recommendations addressed to the state party regarding the measures to be taken to implement the conclusions of GREVIO.

In addition, Article 68(13) of the Convention provides that if GREVIO receives reliable information indicating a situation where problems require immediate attention to prevent or limit the scale or number of serious violations of the Convention, it may request the urgent submission of a special report concerning measures taken to prevent a serious, massive or persistent pattern of violence against women. Under Article 68(14), taking into consideration the information submitted by the state party in question, as well as any other reliable information available to it, GREVIO may designate one or more of its members to conduct an inquiry and to report back urgently to GREVIO. No inquiries have however been carried out as yet. Also, under Article 69, GREVIO may adopt, where appropriate, general recommendations to states on the implementation of the Convention.[9]

As with CEDAW, the main monitoring procedure regarding compliance with the Istanbul Convention is therefore a reporting mechanism. Nevertheless one of the most apparent contrasts between the operation of the monitoring procedures under these two instruments relates to the level of detail involved as regards state reporting on violence against women. All of the reports which states have submitted to GREVIO to date provide extremely in-depth discussion of their responses to violence against women.[10] Such detail is indeed required by the questionnaires which have been developed by GREVIO as the foundation for the evaluation procedures. The comparison between this level of analysis and the amount of information which is provided by states on violence against women in their reports to the CEDAW

9 GREVIO's first General Recommendation was adopted on 20 October 2021 and was on the subject of the digital dimension of violence against women. For further discussion of the monitoring mechanisms under the Convention, see McQuigg, R., *The Istanbul Convention, Domestic Violence and Human Rights*, 2017, Routledge, Abingdon, 110–136; and McQuigg, R., 'Monitoring Mechanism: Commentary on Articles 66–70 of the Istanbul Convention', in De Vido, S. and Frulli, M. (eds.), *Preventing and Combating Violence Against Women and Domestic Violence: A Commentary on the Istanbul Convention*, 2023, Edward Elgar Publishing, Cheltenham, 728.

10 The reports of states parties, the reports formulated by GREVIO in response and the subsequent comments made by states parties on GREVIO's reports are available at https://www.coe.int/en/web/istanbul-convention/country-monitoring-work.

Committee is striking.[11] It is certainly the case that reporting to GREVIO requires the state to undertake a much more considered self-assessment of its response to violence against women than does reporting to the CEDAW Committee. The level of self-assessment required for states to compile a report for submission to GREVIO may in itself be beneficial in terms of contributing towards the effectiveness of state responses to this issue.

In addition, the reports formulated by GREVIO in response to the state reports received crucially provide a far more in-depth assessment than do the Concluding Observations on states' reports which are issued by the CEDAW Committee. Indeed the full Concluding Observations documents, which address numerous issues, are much shorter than the reports by GREVIO which address only violence against women. It is also important to note that to date the procedure used by GREVIO in compiling its reports involves not only a dialogue with state representatives, as is the case with the UN human rights treaty monitoring bodies such as the CEDAW Committee, but also an evaluation visit to each of the states parties in question. The carrying out of such visits by GREVIO is not mandatory under the Istanbul Convention – Article 68(9) simply provides for the organisation by GREVIO of country visits if the information otherwise obtained is insufficient. However, as country visits by GREVIO are taking place as part of the first two evaluation procedures, it is likely that this trend will continue. Again this would seem to be a positive element, in that visiting the state affords GREVIO the opportunity to gain a fuller picture than that which can be obtained through other means.

Another interesting aspect of the reporting procedure under the Istanbul Convention is the fact that the state party in question submits comments on the report by GREVIO, and these comments are published at the same time as GREVIO's report. This is not the normal practice as regards state reactions to reports by the UN human rights treaty monitoring bodies such as CEDAW. From an analysis of the comments submitted by states to date, it seems that states parties will adopt fairly diverse approaches to the style and format of such comments. For example, in the context of the first evaluation procedure, Austria took each of the proposals and suggestions of GREVIO in turn and provided comments on each. Montenegro also commented on each of the areas identified by GREVIO as requiring improvement. Albania provided comments on only a selection of GREVIO's recommendations, while Denmark focused on responding to the aspects of GREVIO's analysis more broadly with which the state disagreed. Sweden used its comments as an opportunity to address aspects of GREVIO's report which it felt were unclear, incomplete or partially inaccurate. By contrast, the comments of states such as Finland, the Netherlands,

11 The periodic reports by states parties to the CEDAW Committee are available from https://www.ohchr.org/en/hrbodies/cedaw/pages/cedawindex.aspx (Office of the High Commissioner for Human Rights).

Serbia, Monaco and Portugal were much briefer. In addition to differences in the format and style of the comments submitted by states parties, there are also notable divergences in terms of the tone adopted. For example, Albania's comments were largely accepting of GREVIO's recommendations, while the comments by Austria were of a more robust nature. While there were certainly many aspects of GREVIO's analysis which were accepted by Austria, the state was also direct in its outright rejection of a number of the suggestions made by GREVIO. Denmark's comments were also robust in their express disagreement with GREVIO's report in particular aspects. Nevertheless, despite the variation in the approaches taken by states parties to providing comments on GREVIO's reports, it seems that the provision of such is a useful exercise in that it gives an immediate indication of the responses of states parties to the proposals and suggestions made by GREVIO.

Another difference between the reporting procedures under CEDAW and under the Istanbul Convention is the involvement of the Committee of the Parties with the latter. With the reporting mechanisms under the current UN treaty monitoring bodies, the Concluding Observations of the latter are essentially the final documents issued to the states in question. However, under the Istanbul Convention, the proposals and suggestions made by GREVIO are then considered by the Committee of the Parties, which in turn makes recommendations to the state concerned. In this respect, an analogy can be drawn with the role of the Committee of Ministers of the Council of Europe in relation to the Advisory Committee on the Framework Convention for the Protection of National Minorities, in that the former makes recommendations based on the latter's reports.[12] Although states are required to implement all of the proposals and suggestions made by GREVIO, the recommendations of the Committee of the Parties are fewer in number and focus on the areas which are highlighted by GREVIO as necessitating urgent or more immediate action. States parties are requested to report back to the Committee after three years on the measures taken to implement these recommendations. On the basis of the information provided by parties and any further information obtained from civil society groups and national institutions for the protection of human rights, the Committee adopts conclusions on the implementation by the state in question of the recommendations. These conclusions may include encouraging the state to take further measures to secure better implementation of the recommendations; and the state is invited to report back within two years on measures taken to this end.[13]

12 See Articles 24(1) and 26(1) of the Framework Convention for the Protection of National Minorities.

13 The recommendations of the Committee of the Parties, the state reports on the implementation of these recommendations, the Committee's conclusions on the implementation of the recommendations and the follow-up reports by states are available at https://www.coe.int/en/web/istanbul-convention/country-monitoring-work.

The fact that the Committee of the Parties is comprised of representatives of the states parties to the Istanbul Convention may serve to place additional pressure on states to comply with the recommendations made to them, more so than if recommendations were simply made by GREVIO without further authorisation by any additional body, such as is the case with the recommendations of the UN treaty monitoring bodies such as the CEDAW Committee. In relation to the Framework Convention for the Protection of National Minorities, De Beco and Lantschner comment that the resolutions of the Committee of Ministers have strengthened the opinions of the Advisory Committee 'by providing them with political backing'.[14]

It is certainly the case that the reporting procedure under the Istanbul Convention is much more detailed than that which operates under UN treaties such as CEDAW. However, whilst this clearly has advantages, there are also problems entailed with such an approach. In particular, the process is undeniably very time-consuming from the perspectives of both the monitoring bodies and the states parties in question. The timetable adopted by GREVIO for completing the initial round of reporting as regards all of the states parties to the Convention was therefore unavoidably of a somewhat protracted nature. For the initial monitoring procedure, the entire process, from a state being sent the baseline questionnaire to the state reporting back following the adoption by the Committee of the Parties of conclusions on the implementation of its recommendations, took in excess of seven years. During this time, the state submitted four reports or sets of comments; and the monitoring bodies issued three reports or sets of recommendations or conclusions, as well as GREVIO undertaking an evaluation visit to the state in question. Also, during the initial monitoring procedure, GREVIO usually only sent the baseline questionnaire to two or three states parties at any one time. Given the very detailed monitoring procedure involved, it is of course understandable that GREVIO adopted such a gradual approach to monitoring. Indeed, asking a large number of states to submit the questionnaire at the same time would simply have made the process unworkable, as GREVIO would not have had the time or resources to deal with the workload involved. Nevertheless, this approach meant that states had generally been parties to the Istanbul Convention for around four years before they were required to submit their first report to GREVIO. By comparison, all states parties to CEDAW for example are required to submit an initial report within two years of ratifying this instrument.[15] Four or five states parties at any one time are being sent the questionnaire on which the second

14 De Beco, G. and Lantschner, E., 'The Advisory Committee on the Framework Convention for the Protection of National Minorities (the ACFC)', in De Beco, G. (ed.), *Human Rights Monitoring Mechanisms of the Council of Europe*, 2012, Routledge, Abingdon, 100 at 119.

15 Article 18(a) of CEDAW.

monitoring procedure in respect of the Istanbul Convention is based, which demonstrates an approach which has been accelerated, but only to a limited extent.

As with the Istanbul Convention, the adoption of a stand-alone UN treaty on violence against women with its own monitoring body would allow greater scope for in-depth evaluation of state compliance and for the incorporation of innovative variations on the traditional reporting procedure. It is true that the gradual approach adopted by GREVIO and the Committee of the Parties is likely to be successful in avoiding the difficulties involving backlogs of reports which have proven to be so problematic for the UN human rights treaty monitoring bodies, such as the CEDAW Committee. The timetable for monitoring state compliance with the Istanbul Convention has obviously been thought out in a very considered manner with these difficulties clearly in mind. However, despite the possible advantages of the adoption of such a gradual approach to reporting in terms of the avoidance of delays and also as regards the level of detail of the assessment involved, it is nevertheless extremely unlikely that the use of such an approach would be possible for a global human rights treaty monitoring body for purely practical reasons. It must be remembered that, as a regional human rights instrument, the Istanbul Convention currently has only 38 states parties, whereas it is probable that a global treaty on violence against women would have a considerably greater number of states parties. For example, there are 189 states which are party to CEDAW. In the context of a new UN treaty on violence against women with potentially a similar number of states parties, the type of in-depth assessment currently being performed by GREVIO and the Committee of the Parties would be unlikely to be feasible. If a monitoring body attached to such an instrument were to adopt a similarly gradual approach to reporting, it simply would not be possible to get through all of the states parties in question in any type of reasonable timeframe. It is very improbable that a new UN treaty monitoring body would have the time or resources to visit each state party upon receipt of the report from that state or indeed to make such detailed recommendations to each state as are being made by GREVIO. It is also very unlikely, were a stand-alone UN treaty on violence against women with its own monitoring body to be adopted, that a body with a similar role to that of the Committee of the Parties would be established, given that none of the existing UN human rights treaty monitoring mechanisms include such a body.

Although it is unlikely that the very thorough approach to monitoring state compliance with the Istanbul Convention could be replicated at the global level, the fact remains nevertheless that a monitoring body focused solely on violence against women as established under a new stand-alone UN treaty on this issue would be able to assess compliance in a more detailed manner than the CEDAW Committee could assess compliance with a new Optional Protocol to CEDAW. Also, if legally binding provisions on violence against women were to take the form of an Optional Protocol to CEDAW, this would make it very likely that the monitoring process in respect of state compliance with these provisions would simply replicate that of CEDAW itself, with all the attendant problems which currently exist.[16] However, the adoption of a new UN treaty on violence against women would allow for significantly greater flexibility in terms of the monitoring mechanisms which would pertain to such an instrument, even if the type of monitoring process utilised in respect of the Istanbul Convention would not be realistic. It is likely that the monitoring mechanisms of a UN treaty on violence against women would follow broadly the same form as those of the other UN human rights treaties, with a reporting mechanism constituting the primary method of monitoring compliance, along with a (potentially optional) communications mechanism and inquiry procedure. There are nonetheless a number of innovative measures relevant to monitoring which have been adopted under the more recent UN human rights treaties, such as the UN Convention on the Rights of Persons With Disabilities (CRPD),[17] which may also be advantageous in the context of a treaty on violence against women. For example, under Article 36(2) of the CRPD, if a report is 'significantly overdue', the Committee on the Rights of Persons With Disabilities may give the state party a three-month notice to submit a report. Another innovation relates to the Conference of States Parties. Article 40 of the CRPD provides for periodic meetings of states parties to assess the implementation of the Convention. While previous human rights treaties did refer to meetings of states parties, these mechanisms were intended to be used for purposes relevant to the election of Committee members or amendments to the treaties in question, as opposed to wider functions. Such meetings in the context of the CRPD are meant to facilitate implementation by drawing together a broad range of actors, including states parties, non-governmental organisations and relevant UN agencies, in order to discuss how best to ensure the implementation of the CRPD.[18]

Conclusion

In conclusion, it is true that using the vehicle of the adoption of an Optional Protocol to CEDAW to put in place legally binding standards at the global level on violence against women would have significant merits. For instance, this course of action would be likely to be considerably less costly than the adoption of a stand-alone UN treaty and the establishment of a separate monitoring body. In addition, an Optional Protocol to CEDAW would involve

16 Further discussion of these difficulties can be found in Chapter Three.

17 The CRPD and its Optional Protocol were adopted in 2006.

18 For further discussion, see Stein, M.A. and Lord, J.E., 'Monitoring the Convention on the Rights of Persons with Disabilities: Innovations, Lost Opportunities, and Future Potential' (2010) 32 *Human Rights Quarterly* 689.

less of a reporting burden for states, in that states parties to such a Protocol could include information on compliance within their reports to the CEDAW Committee on their implementation of CEDAW more generally. This may in turn encourage more states to ratify such an instrument. Also, given that the current and former Special Rapporteurs on violence against women have now expressed their support for an Optional Protocol to CEDAW on violence against women, it is now very unlikely that the more radical alternative of a stand-alone UN treaty on violence against women would be adopted.

Nevertheless, as was discussed in this chapter, the adoption of an Optional Protocol to CEDAW, as opposed to a stand-alone treaty, could carry significant disadvantages. For instance, given the pressures under which the CEDAW Committee works, it is difficult to see how this Committee could undertake any additional burden of monitoring. By contrast, a new treaty monitoring body focused exclusively on the issue of violence against women would be able to monitor compliance in a significantly more in-depth manner than would the CEDAW Committee, the capacity of which is already over-stretched. Although it is probable that states which would be parties to both a UN treaty on violence against women and to CEDAW would still be required to include information on their responses to violence against women in their periodic reports to the CEDAW Committee, it is very unlikely that this would constitute any real inconvenience for such states. Indeed the CEDAW Committee itself has regularly urged states within the Council of Europe not yet parties to the Istanbul Convention to ratify this instrument, thereby encouraging such states to take on a similar reporting obligation as that which would be entailed by becoming party to a UN treaty on violence against women.

Essentially the adoption of a stand-alone treaty on violence against women with its own monitoring body would allow for much more detailed scrutiny of state responses to this issue. This point is brought into particularly sharp focus when a comparison is made between monitoring of state compliance with the Istanbul Convention and the monitoring of state responses to violence against women as carried out by the CEDAW Committee. Although it is unlikely that the very thorough approach to monitoring state compliance with the Istanbul Convention could be replicated at the global level, it is nevertheless the case that a monitoring body focused solely on violence against women would be able to assess compliance in a more detailed manner than the CEDAW Committee, the capacity of which is already over-stretched, could assess compliance with a new Optional Protocol to CEDAW. Also, if legally binding provisions on violence against women were to take the form of an Optional Protocol to CEDAW, this would make it very probable that the monitoring process in respect of state compliance with these provisions would simply replicate that of CEDAW itself, with all the attendant problems which currently exist. However, the adoption of a new UN treaty on violence against women would allow for considerably greater flexibility in terms of the monitoring mechanisms which would pertain to such an instrument.

6 Conclusions

This book has sought to provide a detailed analysis of the international legal framework on violence against women and, crucially, the need for reform of this framework. Although violence against women is one of the most prevalent human rights abuses at the global level, none of the UN treaties refer specifically to this issue. The book has argued that this omission is no longer acceptable and that there is a strong need for reform of the international framework on violence against women. In terms of the form which such change should take, the ideal course of action would be the adoption of a stand-alone treaty at the UN level on this issue. However, it is recognised that such a development may not be achievable for reasons of practicality, such as the resources which would be entailed and lack of political will. It is therefore argued that, despite the potential difficulties involved, the adoption of an Optional Protocol to CEDAW on violence against women would be a very meritorious development in terms of reforming the international legal framework on this issue.

As was discussed in Chapter Two, the omission from CEDAW of express reference to violence against women can be explained by the fact that this instrument was adopted 45 years ago, at a time when there was less understanding of the importance and prevalence of such violence. Also, human rights were originally formulated in such a manner as to create a 'public/private divide', whereby rights were deemed to be applicable in the 'public' sphere where the state was directly involved, but were not deemed to apply in the 'private' sphere in situations involving only private individuals. As the majority of violence against women occurs in the 'private' sphere, the existence of the public/private dichotomy meant that such violence was largely excluded from the rights discourse. Although concepts of state responsibility and positive obligations have now been developed which enable human rights to enter the 'private' sphere, such concepts were still in their infancy at the time of the drafting of CEDAW. In addition, although CEDAW has been described as an international bill of rights for women, technically the aim of this instrument was to combat discrimination against women, as opposed to securing the rights of women more substantively. At the time of the drafting

DOI: 10.4324/9781003603689-6

of CEDAW, violence against women was not generally viewed as a matter relating to gender-based discrimination.

Nevertheless, despite the omission from CEDAW of any express reference to violence against women, the CEDAW Committee has in its General Recommendations Nos. 19 and 35 interpreted this instrument in such a way as to encompass this issue.[1] Other UN bodies have also addressed the subject of violence against women. For example, the UN General Assembly has passed Resolutions on this issue, including the UN Declaration on the Elimination of Violence Against Women.[2] Resolutions relating to violence against women were also issued by the Commission on Human Rights[3] and have been issued by the Human Rights Council, which replaced the Commission on Human Rights in 2006.[4] In addition, violence against women was addressed in the Vienna Declaration and Programme of Action which was adopted by the World Conference on Human Rights in Vienna in June 1993. Indeed the importance which is accorded by the UN bodies to this subject is seen in the very existence of the office of the Special Rapporteur on violence against women, its causes and consequences. Since the inception of this post in 1994, those who have held the office have issued a multitude of detailed reports. In addition, the Beijing Declaration and Platform for Action which was issued following the Fourth World Conference on Women organised by the UN which took place in 1995, contained detailed recommendations on the measures which states should adopt in order to address violence against women.[5]

Given the extensive consideration of violence against women which is afforded by the CEDAW Committee and also other UN bodies, Chapter Three analysed why reform of the international legal framework on this issue is nevertheless necessary. Although a multitude of statements have been issued by

1 Committee on the Elimination of Discrimination Against Women, General Recommendation No. 19, U.N. Doc. A/47/38 (1992); and Committee on the Elimination of Discrimination Against Women, General Recommendation No. 35 on gender-based violence against women, updating General Recommendation No. 19, CEDAW/C/GC/35 (2017).

2 General Assembly Resolution A/RES/48/104, 20 December 1993. See also for example, the Resolutions of the General Assembly on intensification of efforts to eliminate all forms of violence against women which were adopted on 19 December 2006 (A/RES/61/143); 18 December 2007 (A/RES/62/133); 18 December 2008 (A/RES/63/155); 18 December 2009 (A/RES/64/137); 21 December 2010 (A/RES/65/187); 20 December 2012 (A/RES/67/144).

3 See for example Commission on Human Rights Resolution E/CN.4/RES/2001/49, 23 April 2001; Commission on Human Rights Resolution E/CN.4/RES/2004/46, 20 April 2004.

4 See for example Resolution 7/24 (2008) 'Elimination of Violence Against Women'; Resolution 11/2 (2009) 'Accelerating Efforts to Eliminate All Forms of Violence Against Women'; Resolution 14/12 (2010) 'Accelerating Efforts to Eliminate All Forms of Violence Against Women: Ensuring Due Diligence in Prevention'; Resolution 20/12 (2012) 'Accelerating Efforts to Eliminate All Forms of Violence Against Women: Remedies for Women Who Have Been Subjected to Violence'.

5 Beijing Platform for Action, U.N. Doc. A/CONF. 177/20 (1995).

the CEDAW Committee and by other UN bodies on violence against women, these all fall within the category of 'soft law' which is non-binding on states. It is problematic from the perspective of principle that there are no legally binding provisions on this issue at the global level. Since CEDAW was adopted in 1979, there have been enormous developments in the understanding of violence against women, and it is no longer tenable for the lack of UN treaty provisions on this subject to remain unaddressed. Such provisions would have a symbolic value and would add considerably more force to the statements made by the CEDAW Committee and the other UN human rights bodies as regards this issue.

The lack of legally binding provisions at the UN level on violence against women is also problematic from a practical perspective. Although there are of course considerable difficulties with the implementation of human rights standards, it is argued that the existence of such standards make a significant difference as regards how states respond to particular issues. It is also contended that human rights standards need to be legally binding in order for them to attain a sufficient degree of efficacy. Indeed, it is notable that in 2011 the Council of Europe adopted the Istanbul Convention and that in 2025 the African Union adopted the Convention on Ending Violence Against Women and Girls, despite the fact that all of the member states of both the Council of Europe and the AU were already parties to CEDAW and were thus subject to the 'soft law' standards developed by the CEDAW Committee and the other UN bodies in this area. Few of the measures found among the provisions of the Istanbul Convention or the AU Convention were new – most had been previously articulated by the CEDAW Committee and other UN bodies. However, the Council of Europe and the AU nevertheless saw fit to put these standards in the format of treaties, thereby making them legally binding. If the Council of Europe or the AU had been of the view that it did not matter whether these standards were 'soft law' or legally binding, there would have been very little point in adopting these instruments.

It is also argued that the fact that there are a number of legally binding provisions on violence against women within the context of regional systems of human rights protection does not eliminate the necessity for legally binding provisions at the global level on this issue. There are huge swathes of the globe which do not fall within any of the regional systems of human rights protection which encompass treaty provisions on violence against women. Also, the regional provisions on this issue vary considerably in their scope. For example, whilst the Istanbul Convention places extremely detailed duties on states parties, the AU Convention and the Convention of Belém do Pará place far less detailed obligations on states. There is thus a need for a uniform set of duties to be adopted.

The book then proceeded to examine the form which should be taken by such legally binding provisions at the UN level on violence against women. One possibility would be the adoption of an Optional Protocol to CEDAW on this issue, as was discussed in Chapter Four. In December 2023, the current UN Special Rapporteur on violence against women, its causes and consequences, Reem Alsalem, along with two previous holders of this mandate, Dubravka Šimonović and Rashida Manjoo, issued a joint call for states to consider strongly the adoption of such an Optional Protocol.[6] In terms of advancing the debate on the need for the adoption of legally binding standards at the global level on violence against women, it is advantageous that the current Special Rapporteur, along with two former Special Rapporteurs, have adopted an agreed position on the form which such legally binding standards should take. The fact that the current and former Special Rapporteurs are presenting a unified front on this issue may well serve to advance the chances of legally binding standards being adopted.

The adoption of an Optional Protocol to CEDAW on violence against women to be monitored by the CEDAW Committee certainly has notable attractions, as this course of action would be considerably less costly than the adoption of a stand-alone treaty and the establishment of a separate monitoring body. Also, this approach would carry less of a reporting burden for states, in that parties to such a Protocol could include information on compliance within their reports to the CEDAW Committee on their implementation of CEDAW more generally. This may in turn encourage more states to ratify such an instrument. In addition, the existence of the CEDAW Committee's General Recommendation No. 35 on gender-based violence would mean that there would be an initial blueprint from which to work in terms of drafting such an Optional Protocol. The fact that the CEDAW Committee already refers to General Recommendation No. 35 when assessing state compliance with CEDAW may also encourage states to ratify an Optional Protocol based on this General Recommendation, given that they would already have a level of familiarity with the provisions contained therein.

It is however arguable that the adoption of an Optional Protocol to CEDAW would not be the most effective method of achieving the goal of implementing legally binding standards at the global level on violence against women. In particular, given the pressures under which the CEDAW Committee works, it is difficult to see how this body could undertake any additional burden of monitoring. Chapter Five therefore analysed another form which legally binding provisions at the UN level on violence against women could take, namely a stand-alone treaty with its own monitoring body. Crucially, a new treaty monitoring body focused exclusively on the issue of violence against women would be able to monitor compliance in a considerably more detailed

6 Statement by current and former Special Rapporteurs on violence against women, its causes and consequences, 'Now Is the Time for an Optional Protocol to CEDAW on Violence Against Women and Girls', 7 December 2023, available at https://www.ohchr.org/sites/default/files/documents/issues/women/sr/statements/stm-op-vaw-sr-vaw-7-12-23.pdf.

manner than would the CEDAW Committee, the capacity of which is already over-stretched. Although it is probable that states which would be parties to both a UN treaty on violence against women and to CEDAW would still be required to include information on their responses to violence against women in their periodic reports to the CEDAW Committee, it is improbable that this would constitute any real inconvenience for such states. Indeed the CEDAW Committee itself has regularly urged states within the Council of Europe to ratify the Istanbul Convention, thereby encouraging such states to take on a similar reporting obligation as that which would be entailed by becoming party to a UN treaty on violence against women.

Essentially the adoption of a stand-alone treaty on violence against women with its own monitoring body would allow for substantially more detailed scrutiny of state responses to this issue. This point is brought into particularly sharp focus when a comparison is made between monitoring of state compliance with the Istanbul Convention and the monitoring of state responses to violence against women as carried out by the CEDAW Committee, as was discussed in Chapter Five. Although it is unlikely for reasons of practicality that the very thorough approach to monitoring of state compliance with the Istanbul Convention could be replicated at the global level, it is nevertheless the case that a monitoring body focused solely on violence against women would be able to assess compliance in a much more in-depth manner than the CEDAW Committee, the capacity of which is already over-stretched, could assess compliance with a new Optional Protocol to CEDAW. Also, if legally binding provisions on violence against women were to take the form of an Optional Protocol to CEDAW, this would make it very probable that the monitoring process in respect of state compliance with these provisions would simply replicate that of CEDAW itself, with all the attendant problems which currently exist. However, the adoption of a new UN treaty on violence against women would allow for considerably greater flexibility in terms of the monitoring mechanisms which would pertain to such an instrument and for the incorporation of innovative variations on traditional reporting procedures.

This book has argued that, in terms of achieving the optimal level of effectiveness of legally binding standards at the UN level on violence against women, it would be best for such standards to be implemented in the form of a new stand-alone treaty on this issue. It is nevertheless recognised that, given that the current UN Special Rapporteur on violence against women, and two previous holders of this role, have expressed their support for an Optional Protocol to CEDAW on violence against women, it is now very unlikely that the more radical alternative of a stand-alone instrument would be adopted. As was discussed in Chapter Five, it is possible that the decision of the current and former Special Rapporteurs to support the format of an Optional Protocol to CEDAW for legally binding provisions at the UN level on violence against women may have been due, at least partly, to political considerations, rather than necessarily to a belief that the vehicle of an Optional Protocol would be the best way of achieving the highest possible level of effectiveness of such provisions. In particular, the support of the CEDAW Committee for an Optional Protocol may be significantly easier to gain than would the support of this Committee for a new stand-alone treaty. Given the crucial role which the CEDAW Committee plays internationally in the protection of the rights of women, the support of this body would undoubtedly be vital to the success of any proposal to adopt legally binding standards at the global level on violence against women. Indeed, it is very unlikely that states could be persuaded to ratify an instrument containing legally binding provisions on this issue if such an instrument did not enjoy the support of the CEDAW Committee.

Nevertheless, even though an Optional Protocol to CEDAW on violence against women does not offer the same opportunities for innovative monitoring methods or in-depth scrutiny of state compliance as would a stand-alone treaty with its own monitoring body, the potential significance of such an Optional Protocol should not be underestimated. The adoption of such an instrument would have tremendous symbolic value in terms of a recognition at the international level of the prevalence and importance of the issue of violence against women and of the urgent need for further steps to be taken to address this issue. Such an Optional Protocol would also add substantially more force to the statements made by the CEDAW Committee and the other UN human rights bodies as regards violence against women. Although the ideal way forward may have been the adoption of a stand-alone treaty, idealism must at times give way to realism and to a recognition that compromise may be necessary. To that end, it is to be hoped that the UN bodies and states parties will work together to develop and implement an Optional Protocol to CEDAW on violence against women.

Bibliography

Afsharipour A., 'Empowering Ourselves: The Role of Women's NGOs in the Enforcement of the Women's Convention' (1999) 99 *Columbia Law Review* 129.

Armatta, J., 'Getting Beyond the Law's Complicity in Intimate Violence Against Women' (1997) 33 *Willamette Law Review* 774.

Bayefsky, A.F., *The UN Human Rights Treaty System: Universality at the Crossroads*, 2001, Transnational Publishers, Ardsley.

Bilder, R.B., 'Beyond Compliance: Helping Nations Cooperate', in Shelton, D. (ed.), *Commitment and Compliance: The Role of Non-Binding Norms in the International Legal System*, 2003, Oxford University Press, Oxford, 65.

Binion, G., 'Human Rights: A Feminist Perspective' (1995) 17 *Human Rights Quarterly* 509.

Bond, J.E., 'International Intersectionality: A Theoretical and Pragmatic Exploration of Women's International Human Rights Violations' (2003) 52 *Emory Law Journal* 71.

Bourlet, A., *Police Intervention in Marital Violence*, 1990, Open University Press, Milton Keynes.

Bruce, E., 'Attitudes of Social Workers and Police in the Select Committee Report on Violence to Women and Children', in *Women and Abused Children – Intricacies of Legal and Administrative Intervention*, 1979, Issues Publications, University of Bradford, 50.

Bunch, C., 'Women's Rights as Human Rights: Towards a Re-Visioning of Human Rights' (1990) 12 *Human Rights Quarterly* 486.

Burton, M., *Legal Responses to Domestic Violence*, 2008, Routledge-Cavendish, Abingdon.

Burton, M., 'The Human Rights of Victims of Domestic Violence: *Opuz v Turkey*' (2010) 22 *Child and Family Law Quarterly* 131.

Byrnes, A., 'Enforcement Through International Law and Procedures', in Cook, R.J. (ed.), *Human Rights of Women – National and International Perspectives*, 1994, University of Pennsylvania Press, Philadelphia, 189.

Byrnes, A., 'The Convention on the Elimination of All Forms of Discrimination Against Women', in Benedek, W., Mayambala Kisaakye, E. and Oberleitner, G. (eds.), *Human Rights of Women: International Instruments and African Experiences*, 2002, Palgrave, New York, 119.

Cassel, D., 'Does Human Rights Law Make a Difference?' (2001) 2 *Chicago Journal of International Law* 121.

Charlesworth, H., 'What Are "Women's International Human Rights"?', in Cook, R.J. (ed.), *Human Rights of Women – National and International Perspectives*, 1994, University of Pennsylvania Press, Philadelphia, 58.

Charlesworth, H. and Chinkin, C., *The Boundaries of International Law: A Feminist Analysis*, 2000, Manchester University Press, Manchester.

Charlesworth, H., Chinkin, C. and Wright, S., 'Feminist Approaches to International Law' (1991) 85 *American Journal of International Law* 613.

Charney, J.L., 'Compliance With International Soft Law' in Shelton, D. (ed.), *Commitment and Compliance: The Role of Non-Binding Norms in the International Legal System*, 2003, Oxford University Press, Oxford, 115.

Chinkin, C., 'Violence Against Women', in Freeman, M.A., Chinkin, C. and Rudolf, B. (eds.), *The UN Convention on the Elimination of All Forms of Discrimination Against Women – A Commentary*, 2012, Oxford University Press, Oxford, 443.

Chinkin, C. and Freeman, M.A., 'Introduction', in Freeman, M.A., Chinkin, C. and Rudolf, B. (eds.), *The UN Convention on the Elimination of All Forms of Discrimination Against Women – A Commentary*, 2012, Oxford University Press, Oxford, 2.

Cook, R.J., 'Reservations to the Convention on the Elimination of All Forms of Discrimination Against Women' (1989–1990) 30 *Virginia Journal of International Law* 643.

Cook, R.J., 'Women's International Human Rights Law: The Way Forward', in Cook, R.J. (ed.), *Human Rights of Women – National and International Perspectives*, 1994, University of Pennsylvania Press, Philadelphia, 3.

Copelon, R., 'Intimate Terror: Understanding Domestic Violence as Torture', in Cook, R.J. (ed.), *Human Rights of Women – National and International Perspectives*, 1994, University of Pennsylvania Press, Philadelphia, 116.

Copelon, R., 'International Human Rights Dimensions of Intimate Violence: Another Strand in the Dialectic of Feminist Lawmaking' (2003) 11 *American University Journal of Gender, Social Policy and the Law* 865.

Crawford, J., 'The UN Human Rights Treaty System: A System in Crisis?', in Alston, P. and Crawford, J. (eds.), *The Future of UN Human Rights Treaty Monitoring*, 2000, Cambridge University Press, Cambridge, 1.

De Beco, G. and Lantschner, E., 'The Advisory Committee on the Framework Convention for the Protection of National Minorities (the ACFC)' in De Beco, G. (ed.), *Human Rights Monitoring Mechanisms of the Council of Europe*, 2012, Routledge, Abingdon, 100.

De Vido, S. and Frulli, M. (eds.), *Preventing and Combating Violence Against Women and Domestic Violence: A Commentary on the Istanbul Convention*, 2023, Edward Elgar Publishing, Cheltenham.

Dobash, R.E. and Dobash, R.P., *Violence Against Wives: A Case Against the Patriarchy*, 1979, Open Books, London.

Dobash, R.E. and Dobash, R.P., *Women, Violence and Social Change*, 1992, Routledge, New York.

Edwards, A., *Violence Against Women Under International Human Rights Law*, 2013, Cambridge University Press, Cambridge.

Edwards S., *Policing 'Domestic' Violence: Women, the Law and the State*, 1989, Sage Publications, London.

Egan, S., *The UN Human Rights Treaty System: Law and Procedure*, 2011, Bloomsbury Professional, Dublin.

Ewing, A.P., 'Establishing State Responsibility For Private Acts of Violence Against Women Under the American Convention on Human Rights' (1995) 26 *Columbia Human Rights Law Review* 751.

Fortin, J., *Children's Rights and the Developing Law*, 2003, Butterworths, London.

Fraser, A.S., 'Becoming Human: The Origin and Development of Women's Human Rights Law' (1999) 21 *Human Rights Quarterly* 853.

Fredman, S., *Human Rights Transformed – Positive Rights and Positive Duties*, 2009, Oxford University Press, Oxford.

Gaer, F.D., 'And Never the Twain Shall Meet? The Struggle to Establish Women's Rights as International Human Rights' in Lockwood, C.E., Magraw, D.B., Spring, M.F. and Strong, S.I. (eds.), *The International Human Rights of Women – Instruments of Change*, 1998, American Bar Association, Washington, DC, 1.

Goodman, R. and Jinks, D., 'Measuring the Effects of Human Rights Treaties' (2003) 14 *European Journal of International Law* 171.

Goodman, R. and Jinks, D., *Socializing States: Promoting Human Rights Through International Law*, 2013, Oxford University Press, New York.

Goodmark, L., 'Symposium: Domestic Violence & the Law: Theory, Policy, and Practice: Law is the Answer? Do We Know that for Sure?: Questioning the Efficacy of Legal Interventions for Battered Women' (2004) 23 *Saint Louis University Public Law Review* 7.

Grdinic, E., 'Application of the Elements of Torture and Other Forms of Ill-Treatment, as Defined by the European Court and Commission of Human Rights, to the Incidents of Domestic Violence' (2000) 23 *Hastings International and Comparative Law Review* 217.

Haas, P.M., 'Choosing to Comply: Theorizing from International Relations and Comparative Politics' in Shelton, D. (ed.), *Commitment and Compliance: The Role of Non-Binding Norms in the International Legal System*, 2003, Oxford University Press, Oxford, 43.

Hafner-Burton, E.M. and Tsutsui, K., 'Human Rights in a Globalizing World: The Paradox of Empty Promises' (2005) 110 *American Journal of Sociology* 1373.

Harvey, C., 'Talking About Human Rights' [2004] *European Human Rights Law Review* 500.

Hathaway, O., 'Do Human Rights Treaties Make a Difference?' (2002) 111 *Yale Law Journal* 1935.

Hathaway, O., 'Testing Conventional Wisdom' (2003) 14 *European Journal of International Law* 185.

Hirschl, R., '"Negative" Rights vs. "Positive" Entitlements: A Comparative Study of Judicial Interpretations of Rights in an Emerging Neo-Liberal Economic Order' (2000) 22 *Human Rights Quarterly* 1060.

Hughes, B., 'Can Domestic Violence be Considered a Violation of Human Rights Law?' (2006) 14 *British Journal of Midwifery* 192.

Ingelse, C., 'Soft Law' (1993) 20 *Polish Yearbook of International Law* 75.

Isa, F.G., 'The Optional Protocol for the Convention on the Elimination of All Forms of Discrimination Against Women: Strengthening the Protection of Women's Human Rights' (2003) 20 *Arizona Journal of International and Comparative Law* 291.

Johnstone, R.L., 'Feminist Influences on the United Nations Human Rights Treaty Bodies' (2006) 28 *Human Rights Quarterly* 148.

Kalin, W., 'Examination of State Reports', in Keller, H. and Ulfstein, G. (eds.), *UN Human Rights Treaty Bodies – Law and Legitimacy*, 2012, Cambridge University Press, Cambridge, 16.

Keith, L.C., 'The United Nations International Covenant on Civil and Political Rights: Does It Make a Difference in Human Rights Behavior?' (1999) 36 *Journal of Peace Research* 95.

Klabbers, J., 'The Redundancy of Soft Law' (1996) 65 *Nordic Journal of International Law* 167.

Knop, K., 'Introduction', in Knop, K. (ed.), *Gender and Human Rights*, 2004, Oxford University Press, Oxford, 1.

Lacey, N., *Unspeakable Subjects*, 1998, Hart Publishing, Oxford.

Lacey, N., 'Feminist Legal Theory and the Rights of Women', in Knop, K. (ed.), *Gender and Human Rights*, 2004, Oxford University Press, Oxford, 13.

Londono, P., 'Developing Human Rights Principles in Cases of Gender-Based Violence: *Opuz v Turkey* in the European Court of Human Rights' (2009) 9 *Human Rights Law Review* 662.

Manjoo, R. and Nadj, D., ' "Bridging the Divide": An Interview With Professor Rashida Manjoo, UN Special Rapporteur on Violence Against Women' (2015) 23 *Feminist Legal Studies* 329.

McCormick, J.M., and Mitchell, N.J., 'Human Rights Violations, Umbrella Concepts, and Empirical Analysis' (1997) 49 *World Politics* 510.

McQuigg, R., 'The Responses of States to the Comments of the CEDAW Committee on Domestic Violence' (2007) 11 *International Journal of Human Rights* 461.

McQuigg, R., 'The CEDAW Committee and Gender-Based Violence Against Women: General Recommendation No. 35' (2017) 6 *International Human Rights Law Review* 263.

McQuigg, R., *International Human Rights Law and Domestic Violence*, 2011, Routledge, Abingdon.

McQuigg, R., 'Is It Time for a UN Treaty on Violence Against Women?' (2018) 22 *International Journal of Human Rights* 305.

McQuigg, R., *The Istanbul Convention, Domestic Violence and Human Rights*, 2017, Routledge, Abingdon.

McQuigg, R., 'Monitoring Mechanism: Commentary on Articles 66–70 of the Istanbul Convention', in De Vido, S. and Frulli, M. (eds.), *Preventing and Combating Violence Against Women and Domestic Violence: A Commentary on the Istanbul Convention*, 2023, Edward Elgar Publishing, Cheltenham, 728.

Merry, S.E., 'Constructing a Global Law – Violence Against Women and the Human Rights System' (2003) 28 *Law and Social Inquiry* 941.

Merry, S.E., *Gender Violence – A Cultural Perspective*, 2009, Wiley-Blackwell, Chichester.

Merry, S.E., *Human Rights and Gender Violence*, 2006, University of Chicago Press, Chicago.
Merry, S.E. (ed.), *The Quiet Power of Indicators: Measuring Governance, Corruption, and Rule of Law*, 2015, Cambridge University Press, Cambridge.
Mowbray, A.R., *The Development of Positive Obligations Under the European Convention on Human Rights by the European Court of Human Rights*, 2004, Hart Publishing, Oxford.
O'Connell, M.E., 'The Role of Soft Law in a Global Order' in Shelton, D. (ed.), *Commitment and Compliance: The Role of Non-Binding Norms in the International Legal System*, 2003, Oxford University Press, Oxford, 100.
O'Hare, U., 'Realising Women's Human Rights' (1999) 21 *Human Rights Quarterly* 364.
Radford, L., 'Legalising Woman Abuse' in Hanmer, J. and Maynard, M. (eds.), *Women, Violence and Social Control*, 1987, Macmillan, London.
Rehman, J., *International Human Rights Law*, 2nd ed., 2010, Pearson Education Limited, Harlow.
Rishmawi, M., 'The Developing Approaches of the International Commission of Jurists to Women's Human Rights', in Cook, R.J. (ed.), *Human Rights of Women – National and International Perspectives*, 1994, University of Pennsylvania Press, Philadelphia, 340.
Risse, T. and Ropp, S.C., 'International Human Rights Norms and Domestic Change: Conclusions', in Risse, T., Ropp, S.C. and Sikkink, K. (eds.), *The Power of Human Rights – International Norms and Domestic Change*, 1999, Cambridge University Press, Cambridge, 234.
Risse, T. and Sikkink, K., 'The Socialization of International Human Rights Norms into Domestic Practices: Introduction', in Risse, T., Ropp, S.C. and Sikkink, K. (eds.), *The Power of Human Rights – International Norms and Domestic Change*, 1999, Cambridge University Press, Cambridge, 1.
Ritz, K.L., 'Soft Enforcement: Inadequacies of Optional Protocol as a Remedy for the Convention on the Elimination of All Forms of Discrimination Against Women' (2001) 25 *Suffolk Transnational Law Review* 191.
Robinson, M., 'Making Human Rights Matter: Eleanor Roosevelt's Time Has Come' (2003) 16 *Harvard Human Rights Journal* 1.
Romany, C., 'Women as Aliens: A Feminist Critique of the Public/Private Distinction in International Human Rights Law' (1993) 6 *Harvard Human Rights Journal* 87.
Schneider, E., *Battered Women & Feminist Lawmaking*, 2000, Yale University Press, Connecticut.
Schopp-Schilling, H.B., 'Treaty Body Reform: The Case of the Committee on the Elimination of Discrimination Against Women' (2007) 7 *Human Rights Law Review* 201.
Shelton, D., 'Commentary and Conclusions', in Shelton, D. (ed.), *Commitment and Compliance: The Role of Non-Binding Norms in the International Legal System*, 2003, Oxford University Press, Oxford, 449.
Simmons, B.A., *Mobilizing for Human Rights: International Law in Domestic Politics*, 2009, Cambridge University Press, New York.
Šimonović, D., 'Global and Regional Standards on Violence Against Women: The Evolution and Synergy of the CEDAW and Istanbul Conventions' (2014) 36 *Human Rights Quarterly* 590.

Smith, L.J.F., 'Domestic Violence: An Overview of the Literature' [1989] *Home Office Research Study* 107.

Smith, R.K.M., *Textbook on International Human Rights*, 6th ed., 2014, Oxford University Press, Oxford.

Stark, B., 'Symposium on Integrating Responses to Domestic Violence' (2001) 47 *Loyola Law Review* 255.

Stein, M.A. and Lord, J.E., 'Monitoring the Convention on the Rights of Persons with Disabilities: Innovations, Lost Opportunities, and Future Potential' (2010) 32 *Human Rights Quarterly* 689.

Sullivan, C.M., 'Using the ESID Model to Reduce Intimate Male Violence Against Women' (2003) 32 *American Journal of Community Psychology* 295.

Thomas, D.Q. and Beasley, M.E., 'Symposium on Reconceptualizing Violence Against Women By Intimate Partners' (1995) 58 *Albany Law Review* 1119.

Ulrich, J., 'Confronting Gender-Based Violence With International Instruments: Is a Solution to the Pandemic Within Reach?' (2000) 7 *Indiana Journal of Global Legal Studies* 629.

Van Leeuwen, F., *Women's Rights Are Human Rights*, 2010, Intersentia, Antwerp.

Wallace, R., *International Human Rights*, 2001, Sweet & Maxwell, London.

Weil, P., 'Towards Relative Normativity in International Law?' (1983) 77 *American Journal of International Law* 413.

Index

For Product Safety Concerns and Information please contact our EU representative GPSR@taylorandfrancis.com Taylor & Francis Verlag GmbH, Kaufingerstraße 24, 80331 München, Germany

Printed and bound by CPI Group (UK) Ltd, Croydon, CR0 4YY

14/09/2026

02216223-0003